ASCHOLASTIC

Handling

SCIENCE
Data

Activities to develop
information-processing skills

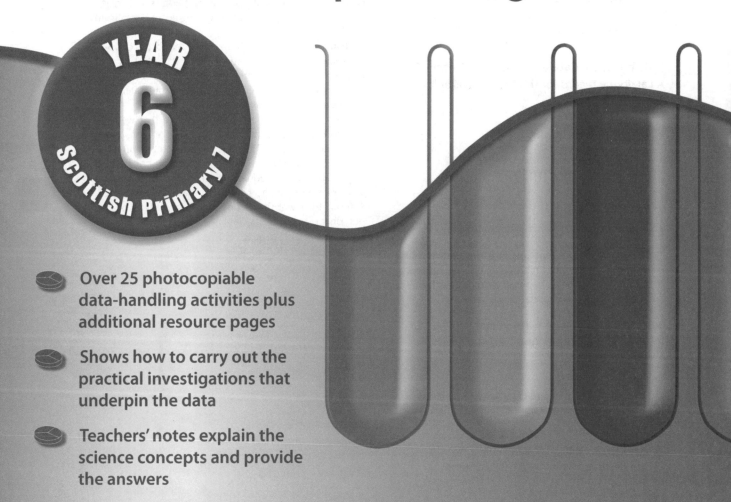

YEAR
6
Scottish Primary 7

- Over 25 photocopiable data-handling activities plus additional resource pages

- Shows how to carry out the practical investigations that underpin the data

- Teachers' notes explain the science concepts and provide the answers

- Ideal for SATs practice

Peter Harwood and Joyce Porter

Authors	Editor	Series designer	Cover illustration
Peter Harwood	Joel Lane	Anna Oliwa	Edward Eaves
Joyce Porter			
	Assistant editor	Designer	Illustrations
	David Sandford	Erik Ivens	Garry Clifford

Text © Peter Harwood and Joyce Porter 2002
© 2002 Scholastic Ltd

Designed using Adobe Pagemaker

Published by Scholastic Ltd,
Villiers House,
Clarendon Avenue,
Leamington Spa,
Warwickshire CV32 5PR

Printed by Bell & Bain Ltd, Glasgow

5 6 7 8 9 0   7 8 9 0 1

British Library Cataloguing-in-Publication Data
A catalogue record for this book is available from the British Library.

ISBN 978-0590-53839-8

Visit our website at www.scholastic.co.uk

Acknowledgements
The authors and publishers wish to thank:

AstraZeneca Science Teaching Trust for their funding and support of the research project on which the activities in this book are based (you can visit the AZSTT website at www.azteachscience.co.uk).

The children of Knowsley, Powys and Trafford LEAs for their help in testing these investigations in the classroom.

The National Curriculum for England 2000
© The Queens Printer and Controller of HMSO.
Reproduced under the terms of HMSO Guidance Note 8.

A Scheme of Work for Key Stages 1 and 2: Science
© Qualifications and Curriculum Authority.
Reproduced under the terms of HMSO Guidance Note 8.

CONTENTS

PAGE	ACTIVITY TITLE	GRAPH TYPE	SCIENCE CURRICULUM REFERENCES		
			QCA UNIT	NATIONAL CURRICULUM	SCOTTISH 5–14 GUIDELINES
10	Food poisoning	Reading block graphs (various scales)	6B	Sc2: 5f	Variety and characteristic features – Level F; Taking responsibility for health: Physical health – Level C
12	Plants in the lawn	Reading a block graph (scale of 2s)	6A	Sc2: 5b, c	Interaction of living things with their environment – Level D
14	Do fertilisers help plants to grow?	Reading line graphs (scale of 1s)	6A	Sc2: 1b; 3a, c	Interaction of living things with their environment – Level D
16	What will I find in the wood?	Interpreting a table of data	6A	Sc1: 1a; Sc2: 1b, c, 5b, c	Interaction of living things with their environment – Level D
18	Investigating bone sizes	Reading a scatter graph	6A	Sc2: 1a, c, 2e	Variety and characteristic features – Level C
20	Compost heap	Reading line graphs (scale of percentage)	6B	Sc2: 5f	Variety and characteristic features – Level E, F
22	Adding yeast to flour	Reading line graphs (scale of 20s)	6B	Sc2: 5f	Variety and characteristic features – Level F
24	Travelling to school	Reading cumulative bar charts	5G/6H	Sc1: 1a; Sc2: 2h, 5a	Interaction of living things with their environment – Level D; Social health – Level D
26	What's in the dustbin?	Reading a pie chart	5G/6H	Sc2: 5a	Interaction of living things with their environment – Level D
28	Dissolving white crystals	Reading a bar chart (scale of 20s)	6C	Sc3: 2a, d; 3b, d	Changing materials – Level C
30	Sugar in hot tea	Reading a line graph (scale of 10s)	6C	Sc3: 2a, c, d	Changing materials – Level E
32	Burning candles	Reading a line graph (scale of 1s)	6D	Sc3: 2f, g	Changing materials – Level D
34	Alka Seltzer	Reading a line graph (scale of 0.1s)	6D	Sc3: 2a, f	Changing materials – Level C
36	Fizz-pop rockets	Reading a line graph (scale of 1s)	6D	Sc3: 2a, f	Changing materials – Level E
38	Weighing water	Reading line graphs (scale of 2s)	6D	Sc3: 2b, c, d	Changing materials – Level C
40	Making toast	Reading a line graph (scale of 2s)	6D	Sc3: 2f, g	Changing materials – Level D
42	Irreversible changes	Reading line graphs (scale of 2s)	6D	Sc3: 2a, f	Changing materials – Level C
44	Better conductors	Reading a block graph (scale of 100s)	6G	Sc4: 1a, b, c	Properties and uses of energy – Level C
46	Longer wires	Reading a stick graph (scale of 0.5s)	6G	Sc4: 1a, b, c	Properties and uses of energy – Level D
48	Lots of batteries	Reading a line graph (scale of 100s)	6G	Sc4: 1a, b, c	Properties and uses of energy – Level D
50	Helicopters	Reading a stick graph (scale of 50s)	6E	Sc4: 2b, c	Forces and their effects – Levels C, D
52	Parachutes	Reading a line graph (scale of 1s)	6E	Sc4: 2c	Forces and their effects – Level E
54	How far the car goes	Interpreting a table of data	6E	Sc4: 2c	Forces and their effects – Levels C, E
56	What should I wear at night?	Reading a block graph (scale of 5s)	6F	Sc4: 3a, c, d	Properties and uses of energy – Level C
58	Shadow puppet	Reading a line graph (scale of 20s)	6F	Sc4: 3a, b	Properties and uses of energy – Level C
60	Light and distance	Interpreting a table of data	6F	Sc4: 1a, 3a	Properties and uses of energy – Level C; Earth in space – Level C

INTRODUCTION

WHY HAVE BOOKS ABOUT HANDLING DATA FOR SCIENCE?

Children's education should provide them with skills that will benefit them for the years to come. Against this background, their ability to read and interpret information from graphs and charts is not only essential for science, but also for everyday life, where children are exposed to information on television, in newspapers and in magazines.

In the early days of the National Curriculum, the APU[1] examined graph work in school science. They found that children could successfully carry out many of the basic skills involved in drawing graphs and extracting information from graphs. However, most of the children failed to look for and describe patterns in their data, and did not understand the wider applications of graphs.

The AKSIS project[2] revisited the use and application of graphs in school science. In their research, they found *'that over 75% of pupils' graphs were incorrectly constructed and most pupils regarded graphs as an end in themselves.'* One of the aims of the project was *'that Scientific Enquiry should develop pupils' understanding of the nature of scientific activity and the relation between data and scientific theories.'*

More recently, the OFSTED subject report on Primary Science (1999–2000) concluded that *'science skills, such as handling data, that draw upon and develop numeracy need to be improved systematically. Pupils are given sufficient opportunity to develop their science through practical activities. However their ability to interpret their results and say what they have found out is sometimes hampered by their lack of understanding of charts and graphs and lack of practice in recognising patterns in data. When they are encouraged to draw their own conclusions and are helped in this by discussion with the teacher, they show better understanding of the science and can apply it in different circumstances.'*

INTRODUCING CHILDREN TO DATA IN SCIENCE

This series of books is timely, then. They have been produced to help children develop their skills in handling data and its interpretation in science. However, these activities came about initially not from a response to OFSTED, but out of a need expressed by teachers. We have undertaken a four-year research programme, 'Developing Excellence in Primary Science', generously funded by the AstraZeneca Science Teaching Trust. This project has involved working with a wide variety of children and teachers. It was not simply an academic research project: it was soundly based in the classroom, with real teachers and real children in real teaching situations.

The research team comprised a group of experienced practitioners in class teaching, and in advisory and academic research, who have worked closely with teachers to address the difficulties of trying to teach science effectively. Working with primary children, alongside their teachers, clearly showed us that there was a need to develop children's data-handling skills in situations that the children were not familiar with. There is a strong tendency for primary children to learn science in a specific context, which can then make it difficult for them to apply their new knowledge to other situations. On seeing a data-handling exercise, children would often respond, 'I haven't done this' – referring to the context, which was not relevant to simply interpreting the data.

An analysis of children's performance in the Key Stage 2 National Tests[3] concurs with the OFSTED report. It shows clearly that children experience considerably more difficulty in applying their knowledge to new situations (a problem of contextualised learning) and in *describing* trends in an acceptable scientific format (although, on further questioning, the children showed an underlying ability to identify trends in data). In this series, both of these aspects

of data handling are addressed, and advice is given to help you develop these skills with your class.

The activities in *Handling Science Data* aim to highlight and provide opportunities to develop those skills that are common to data-handling, as well as showing the children activities that have a practical basis and that are similar, but not necessarily identical, to some they have already done. This should help them to develop the confidence to tackle new scenarios and look primarily at the data itself.

The essential ability to analyse scientific evidence (as highlighted in the OFSTED reports) and to express these ideas scientifically has also been addressed. These are typically the '–er, –er' answers in National Test papers, for example: 'the lar<u>ger</u> the force, the big<u>ger</u> the stretch'. Examples that the children can practise with are given in several of the activities in this book. While children can often recognise a trend in data mentally, they find it difficult to express their ideas in a concise and complete way: a common response would be, for example, 'It gets bigger' (for an elastic material being stretched) – or the children may give very roundabout descriptions from which you might have to extract the trend. To overcome this difficulty, we have devised a writing structure involving a two-line jingle, rather like that of an old-fashioned train, into which the children can fit their response. In this example, the chant would be 'the bigger the force / the greater the stretch.' This focuses the children's ideas; they quickly get used to doing it and are pleased at being able to devise their own jingles. It provides a precise and concise format for expressing their ideas – but they still have to be able to identify the trend.

ABOUT THE *HANDLING SCIENCE DATA* SERIES

HOW THE BOOKS ARE ORGANISED

Each book in this series contains at least 25 activities, each comprising a page of teacher's notes and a photocopiable children's page. Some additional photocopiable resource pages are also provided. Each activity provides data related to the curricula for life processes and living things, materials, and physical processes, together with a set of questions that focus on interpreting the data.

The choice of science topics in this series has primarily been matched to the QCA's *Science Scheme of Work for Key Stage 2*, which many teachers in England are now using. However, the other UK curriculum documents have also been considered, and the teacher's notes give references for the National Curriculum in England, relevant units in the QCA's *Science Scheme of Work* and the Scottish *National Guidelines for Science 5–14*. It is intended that the activities can be used alongside any primary science scheme of work as reinforcement or revision. The level of work has also been matched to the National Numeracy and Literacy Strategies, so that the work is set at an appropriate level with suitable progression for the children in each year group.

FEATURES OF THE PHOTOCOPIABLES

The photocopiable worksheets in each book cater for a range of abilities in relation to graphical interpretation skills. On each sheet, the questions are generally arranged in order of increasing difficulty. Some are deliberately challenging to extend the most able children. The majority of the questions are simply about interpreting the data, so the children need not have done the investigation described in order to be able to answer the questions.

Some of the questions identify the key scientific ideas that are relevant to that investigation. It is hoped that the children will have internalised these key concepts if they have already explored the topic practically. Some questions are deliberately open-ended so they can be used as extension or research exercises, and provide ideal homework material. The questions cover a range of types and include:

- taking readings from graphs
- relating data to properties
- dentifying and predicting trends
- investigative skills
- graph plotting and table design
- science understanding
- visualising an investigation.

The level of language varies between the different activities, and some children may need support with reading some of the worksheets. However, the topics do require technical vocabulary, so it is important that this is introduced and reinforced through any complementary lessons. One way to do this would be to let the children carry out the investigations themselves, and then to use these sheets to provide matching practice or revision material.

The system of notation used for the quoting of units in this series is *factor/ unit*, for example temperature/°C or mass/g. This is the accepted format at all levels of science (and recommended by the ASE), although brackets – temperature (°C) or mass (g) – are acceptable at school ages. It is good practice for children to learn to put units at the top of each column in a table when recording data. This is the mathematical justification for using the '/': everything in the column below is divided by the unit, hence */unit*, and only the numbers need to be written in the columns. Equally, when the children are using spreadsheets, the software will not recognise a cell that contains both text and numbers, so the children need to remember only to use numbers.

FEATURES OF THE TEACHER'S NOTES

We feel strongly that the most valuable way to help the children engage with science is by carrying out activities that provide outcomes (which could be data or observations) around which a class discussion can take place. Almost all of the data presented here has come from actual children's work. These are tried and tested activities, although the nature of practical investigations means that they do not always work as successfully each time. All of the activities carry practical advice on how to carry out the activities that underpin the data. Some of these activities will be familiar to you, others not. Don't be afraid to try them out; the children will respond to them in a positive way, and the data is much more meaningful if it is 'real'.

Even the most experienced and qualified science teachers learn new things all the time; you cannot hope to remember everything you did at school or university (even if you went to all the lectures). Very few primary teachers have the luxury of a post-16 science education, yet they are expected to be in a position to answer a wide range of children's questions. The teacher's notes provided with each activity give the answers to the questions on the worksheets (always useful!), together with the relevant background science associated with the activity. This is to assist you in dealing with questions that, in our experience, the enquiring minds of primary children might come up with, especially if your teaching is open-ended. These notes are not intended to state what you should teach the children about any topic, but to support your knowledge so that you can internalise the concepts and then deal more effectively with the children's ideas.

ABOUT *HANDLING SCIENCE DATA: YEAR 6*

The activities in this book largely follow the topics covered in Year 6 of the QCA's *Science Scheme of Work,* and are also aimed at Level D of the Scottish *National Guidelines for Science 5–14.* The majority of the graphs featured are line graphs. Some bar graphs and 'stick graphs' are included, and these can be used as an intermediate stage between bar graphs and line graphs.

USING COMPUTERS IN PRIMARY SCIENCE LESSONS

Children's confidence in using computers is increasing all the time. So is the availability of computers: most primary classrooms now contain one. Even so, most computer-based learning activities involve either using commercial software that provides children with interactive exercises or using the computer as a research tool. Many teachers are still not confident about using computers as an integral tool for learning science.

Nearly all of the activities in this series are derived from classroom investigations where, in addition to writing the results in an exercise book or a science folder, we have computerised data as a spreadsheet with a graph-plotting facility. The spreadsheet and graph can be used as a method of displaying and, more importantly, analysing the data. Information handling and working with spreadsheets (and databases) is developed throughout the QCA's *ICT Scheme of Work* in Key Stage 2.

If the data is 'live' and on screen, children can predict the effect of changes in results on the appearance of the graph and check it instantaneously. If a result appears anomalous, the correct result can be predicted and inserted into the table and the effect observed immediately in the graph. This develops the skill of identifying trends in data – but at the same time demonstrates the value of careful measurement, which children at this age do not always readily appreciate. When they repeat the result, they will more often than not take more care – if necessary, you can intervene and discuss possible sources of error. This will develop the children's practical skills at the same time.

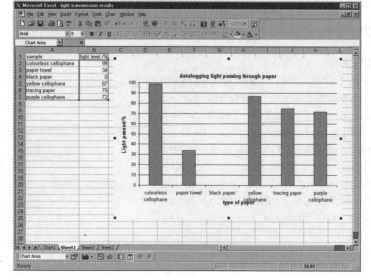

Each book in the series involves some examples of data collected by data-logging. This is a method of using electronic sensors to detect changes in light, temperature and sound, and then storing the data in a form that can be processed using appropriate computer software. This is specifically a feature of the QCA's *ICT Scheme of Work* in Years 5 and 6 (Units 5F and 6C).

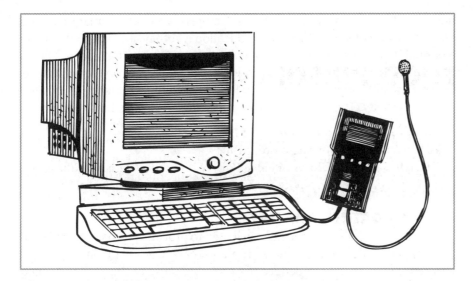

Our research findings, reinforced by our own experiences, suggest that children are much better at interpreting graphs when the data is 'live' – for example, being plotted by the computer as the investigation is carried out.

USEFUL PRACTICAL TECHNIQUES

Adjustable ramps are very useful pieces of equipment for a range of investigations, but commercial ones are normally too expensive for a school to have more than one. Here is a design for a ramp that is cheap and easily made. All you need is some corroflute (corrugated plastic sheeting), string and a spring toggle – then you just follow the instructions below.

Take a length of corroflute and use a craft knife to cut through one surface (along a corrugation, not across), making a hinge. Use a hole punch to make the holes. Attach the string and toggle.

cut one layer of fold

loop of string

corroflute

string

springy toggle
(to grip string
in position)

REFERENCES
1. RM Taylor and P Swatton, *Assessment Matters No.1: Graph Work In School Science* (APU, 1991)
2. A Goldsworthy, R Watson and V Wood Robinson, *Getting to Grips with Graphs, Investigations, Developing Understanding* (ASE, 2000)
3. Standards at Key Stage 2 1996–2000 (QCA, 2001)

FOOD POISONING

National Curriculum Science KS2 PoS Sc2: 5f
QCA Science Unit 6B: Micro-organisms
Scottish 5–14 Guidelines Science Variety and characteristic features –
Level F; Taking responsibility for health: Physical health – Level C

HOW TO GATHER THE DATA

The data shown opposite have been invented to provide a scenario for children to carry out some detective work. The data have been kept simple, so the children should be able to deduce the probable cause of the food poisoning without too much difficulty. You might like to invent a similar scenario, such as workers or college students eating meals in a canteen.

THE SCIENCE BEHIND THE DATA

Data from the Department of Health indicate that half a million people in the UK may be affected by some form of food poisoning each year. It is important that you spend time with the children discussing the basic rules of food safety. This could provide a link to work in design and technology. For instance, you could suggest to your class that they run a French café at lunchtime or break for the rest of the school, and use this to promote food safety. You will need to highlight the differences between cooked foods and raw foods, and the health risks of each.

Of the 100 000 reported cases of food poisoning each year, 58 000 are due to the bacteria *Campylobacter* (this figure is increasing) and 23 000 are due to *Salmonella*. *Campylobacter* passes easily from one food to another through transfer from raw to cooked foods in the fridge, on kitchen work surfaces, via hands and so on. It is destroyed by cooking. These bacteria double in number every 20 minutes or so. If your sandwich contains 1000 bacteria, in 4 hours there will be about 2 million! And in another 4 hours, about 8 billion!

Here are some basic rules for food hygiene. Always wash hands before preparing food and after visiting the toilet. Never lick fingers or utensils and put them back into food. Keep all work surfaces and kitchen cloths very clean. Wash all items (knives, chopping boards) after they have come into contact with raw foods (meat, poultry, eggs), so they do not contaminate cooked foods. Ideally, use different boards and utensils for cooked and fresh food. Keep pets away from food. Wash all food thoroughly (vegetables and fruits). Cook food thoroughly to destroy bacteria. Keep perishable food in the fridge. If cooked and raw food are stored in the fridge, store the cooked food above the raw food so liquids cannot drip onto the cooked food.

Further information can be obtained from the British Nutrition Foundation website: www.nutrition.org.uk (a CD-ROM, *Food Safety for Primary Schools*, is available from this site).

Answers

1. 29
2. 5 (34 – 29)
3. 7
4. 13
5. 13
6. Children who ate a packed lunch.
7. Eating bought sandwiches containing chicken (both chicken salad and chicken tikka).
8. The number who became ill is the same as the number who bought these sandwiches.
9. Bacteria present in the chicken because it had not been cooked properly, someone had not washed their hands properly, or raw food had been stored near the cooked chicken.
10. Wash hands properly, clean all surfaces, cook food thoroughly, keep raw food and cooked food separate in the fridge.

Food poisoning

A party of 30 Year 6 children and four teachers went on a school trip to a science museum. Some of the children had brought packed lunches. On the way there, they stopped at a café where the other children and the teachers bought some sandwiches for lunch. There was a choice of six different types of sandwich. The children and teachers made their selection:

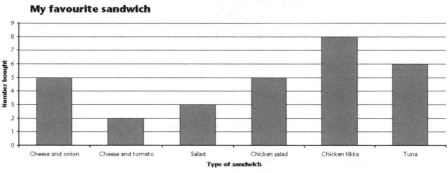

My favourite sandwich

Questions

1. How many sandwiches were bought in total from the café?

2. How many children took packed lunches?

3. How many people had sandwiches with cheese in them?

4. How many people had sandwiches with chicken in them?

In the evening, when they returned from their trip, some children and all the members of staff became ill with severe stomach pains, sickness and diarrhoea – the symptoms of food poisoning.

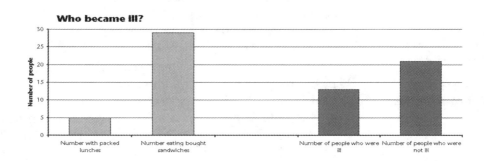

Who became ill?

5. How many people became ill altogether?

6. Which particular group of children do you think did not become ill?

7. What do you think is the most likely cause of the children and teachers becoming ill?

8. Explain how you decided this.

9. What could have contaminated the food?

10. What should people do in their kitchens to handle food safely?

HANDLING SCIENCE DATA YEAR 6

PLANTS IN THE LAWN

National Curriculum Science KS2 PoS Sc2: 5b, c
QCA Science Unit 6A: Interdependence and adaptation
Scottish 5–14 Guidelines Science Interaction of living things with their environment – Level D

HOW TO GATHER THE DATA

Remind the children of previous work on habitats. Revise with them the idea of taking random samples from different parts of the lawn, and why it is better to take several samples from each part of the lawn for comparison. A Year 6 class can be organised into groups to carry out about five quadrat surveys each. Collapsible square quadrats with side length 0.5m can be obtained from most primary science suppliers. It is also possible to construct quadrats from strips of wood or covered wire.

When the children are surveying the lawn, point out the characteristics of each plant: the roots, how the plants are spread and so on (see below).

THE SCIENCE BEHIND THE DATA

You should ask the children what factors may affect the distribution of plant species in the two areas of this habitat. Relevant factors include light intensity, wind, temperature, moisture, acidity, competition, seasonal changes, mowing and people walking on the grass. The children may only suggest some of these, but it is important for them to recognise that the last two factors are probably the most significant in this case. Discuss with them what effects trampling would have on the distribution of plant species in the lawn, and why certain plants are better able to survive being trampled. You could ask them to carry out some research on the different types of plants commonly found in a lawn, using books, CD-ROMs or the Internet.

The plants found in a lawn are adapted to this artificial habitat by being able to reproduce without growing too tall. Each of the plants has significant features that affect its survival in this habitat:

■ **Dandelion:** highly efficient seed dispersal and production, leaves close to the ground, tap root able to produce new leaves even when plant is damaged – so it can survive being trampled on.

■ **Plantain:** leaves close to the ground, broad flat leaves with tough stringy veins resist being trampled on, has a tap root.

■ **Clover:** creeps close to the ground and puts down roots at the same time, but has short roots so will not survive constant trampling.

■ **Daisy:** the rosettes grow very close to the ground, but the roots are not very deep, so does not survive constant trampling well.

■ **Buttercup:** creeps along the surface and puts down roots at the same time, but the roots are short, so does not survive constant trampling.

Answers

1. Grass, daisy, dandelion, plantain.
2. Some of the grass has been worn away by trampling, and the parts of the lawn nearest the path will be bare earth. Trampling damages the grass plants so they don't grow properly.
3. Clover
4. Clover plants are not rooted as deeply as dandelion and plantain plants, and will gradually be removed by trampling.
5. Plantain
6. Plantain plants have long tap roots, and have leaves with tough stringy veins – so the leaves can survive being trampled on, and new leaves will grow if the old leaves are damaged.
7. Three
8. Artificial (though built from natural materials and living things).
9. To obtain a more complete survey of the plants in the lawn. The children looked at ten quadrats, which they placed at random in each habitat. One quadrat might have given results that were not typical (for example, it may have contained a lot of dandelions).
10. Their leaves are close to the ground and they have strong roots, so they can survive when people trample on them.

Plants in the lawn

Children in Year 6 had noticed that the area of lawn near the path leading to school had been worn away by people treading on it. They wanted to find out whether the plants growing near the path were the same as those in the middle of the lawn. They carried out a survey of ten randomly placed square quadrats (of side length 0.5m) in the middle of the lawn. They did the same on the edge of the lawn, close to the path. They recorded the total number of plant species in the ten quadrats in each area and calculated the percentage that each type of plant made up.

They plotted their results as a bar graph, then wrote some useful information about the plants.

Dandelion: efficient seed dispersal, leaves close to the ground, long tap root able to produce new leaves even when plant is damaged.

Plantain: leaves close to the ground, broad flat leaves with tough stringy veins, long tap root.

Clover: creeps along the surface and puts down short roots at the same time.

Daisy: tough leaves grow very close to the ground, roots very strong but not very deep.

Buttercup: creeps along the surface and puts down short roots at the same time.

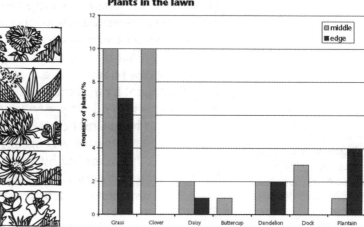

Questions

1. Name the plants that appear in both areas, not just in one.

2. Why is there less grass near the edge of the lawn than in the middle?

3. What is the most common plant (other than grass) found in the middle of the lawn?

4. Why do you think this plant is not found near the edge of the lawn?

5. What is the most common plant (other than grass) near the edge of the lawn?

6. Why do you think this plant survives near the edge where it gets trodden on?

7. How many more plant types were found in the middle of the lawn than at the edge?

8. What kind of habitat is a lawn: is it natural or artificial?

9. Why did the groups carry out ten quadrat surveys of plants in the middle of the lawn and at the edge of the lawn, not just one of each?

10. What do you think were the common features of the plants found near the edge of the lawn?

DO FERTILISERS HELP PLANTS TO GROW?

National Curriculum Science KS2 PoS Sc2: 1b; 3a, c
QCA Science Unit 6A: Interdependence and adaptation
Scottish 5–14 Guidelines Science Interaction of living things with their environment – Level D

HOW TO GATHER THE DATA

This is a difficult activity to carry out, as there will probably be only a small difference in height between the seedlings grown with fertiliser and those grown without. The children need to measure the height of the seedlings accurately to the nearest 0.5cm. They need to calculate the average height of ten seedlings for a reliable comparison, as some seedlings grow better than others. As a control, it is best to use germination sandwiches filled with vermiculite (see photocopiable resource page 64), as there will be no other nutrients present for the control seedlings. If soil or compost were used, there would already be nutrients present anyway, and adding more might not have a significant effect.

Another way of carrying out the activity might be to grow grass seedlings with and without fertiliser for a week and then cut the grass and measure its mass. You can also use data from studies of fields to discuss the use of fertilisers with the children.

THE SCIENCE BEHIND THE DATA

Plants make their own carbohydrates by photosynthesis. However, to make proteins and the pigment chlorophyll (which is essential for photosynthesis), they also need nitrogen. Plants absorb simple nitrogen compounds from the soil; they do not grow well unless there is a plentiful supply of nitrogen, and a nitrogen-rich fertiliser makes lawns much greener. In a natural ecosystem, the nitrogen would normally be released into the soil by rotting plant and animal matter. However, in a garden or field, nitrogen and other elements (phosphorous, sulphur, iron, potassium, calcium, magnesium) can be added in fertiliser. Fertilisers can be organic (manure) or inorganic (such as many of the products bought from garden centres). The latter will usually give you an NPK value, indicating the amount of nitrogen, phosphorus and potassium it contains.

You can explain this to children by saying that a plant needs fertiliser in the same way that humans need vitamins and minerals – reading the names of these from cereal boxes will illustrate the point. Over a longer period, you can demonstrate that pot plants grow better when nutrients are added, or discuss why farmers add fertilisers to their fields. There are environmental issues associated with this: adding inorganic fertilisers does not provide humus, which helps to bind the soil; and the overuse of fertilisers means that nitrates and phosphates run into streams and rivers, endangering human health and upsetting the freshwater ecosystem.

Answers

1. 2cm
2. 6.5cm
3. 7.5cm
4. 1cm
5. 5.5cm
6. 6 days
7. 5.5cm
8. Seedlings grow at different rates; some seedlings grow better than others. Taking the average growth of 10 seedlings allows a more reliable comparison to be made.
9. Several suggestions are possible. The plants did not grow evenly (eg due to variation in temperature or amount of water or light). Incorrect measurement is also possible.
10. If seeds had been planted in the germination sandwich, some of them might not have germinated. By germinating the seeds first, the children can select seedlings of similar size for the investigation. Also, the seed contains nutrients to start the plant off, so all plants will grow initially – but then they must synthesise their own compounds for healthy growth.
11. When farmers harvest crops, they take the nutrients out of the soil. If the same land is used to grow crops every year, it gradually loses nutrients and becomes infertile. Adding fertilisers to the soil puts the nutrients back.

Do fertilisers help plants to grow?

John, Louise and Cathy had germinated some oat seeds; the seedlings had grown to about 2cm in height. The children carefully planted ten of these oat seedlings in a germination sandwich and left them standing in water. They planted ten similar seedlings, but this time they left the germination sandwich standing in some fertiliser that they had bought from the garden centre.

The children carefully measured the seedlings over the course of a week, and worked out the average growth of each set of seedlings each day. They recorded their results as a line graph.

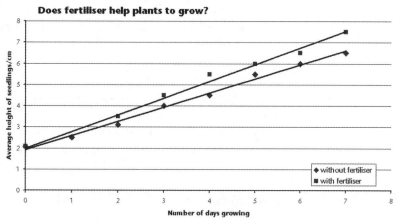

Questions

1. What was the average height of the seedlings at the start?

2. What was the average height of the seedlings without fertiliser after 7 days?

3. What was the average height of the seedlings with fertiliser after 7 days?

4. What was the difference between these two heights?

5. What was the average height of the plants with fertiliser after 4 days?

6. After how many days had the average height of the plants without fertiliser reached 6cm?

7. How much, on average, did the plants with fertiliser grow in the 7 days they were measured?

8. Why do you think the children worked out the average height of 10 seedlings in each set instead of just growing one seedling with fertiliser and one without?

9. The lines the children drew are called 'lines of best fit'. Can you think of a reason why not all the points are on the line in each case?

10. Why did the children use 2cm seedlings to start with instead of ungerminated seeds?

11. Why do farmers add fertilisers to their soil?

HANDLING SCIENCE DATA YEAR 6

WHAT WILL I FIND IN THE WOOD?

> **National Curriculum Science** KS2 PoS Sc1: 1a; Sc2: 1b, 1c, 5b, 5c
> **QCA Science** Unit 6A: Interdependence and adaptation
> **Scottish 5–14 Guidelines Science** Interaction of living things with their environment – Level D

HOW TO GATHER THE DATA

If there is some woodland near the school, you can take the children on a visit and ask them to record the living things that they see. They can make a tally chart of how many of each species they see, as well as drawings of the key features of each. Remember that flowers such as bluebells are protected species and the children should not pick them. If you are able to visit at different times of year, you can build up a detailed picture of the habitat and how it changes. When the children return to school, they can research the living things they have seen using books, CD-ROMs and the Internet. The website www.uksafari.com has some information that is easily accessible to primary school children, and has good links to other sites.

THE SCIENCE BEHIND THE DATA

You can use this activity to talk about how living things adapt to their habitat and about daily and seasonal changes in their habitat. Most animals and plants are more active during the day. What living things would the children see in the day? When would they expect to see the owl? Flowers are usually open during daylight to attract insects, but close at night. Some nocturnal animals (such as owls) hunt at night: their eyesand ears are specially adapted to see small animals moving in dim light.

You can also discuss how animals and plants survive during the winter months. Annual plants die after making seeds to survive the winter; perennial plants, such as bulbs (bluebells) and trees, can survive for many years by losing their leaves in winter and growing new ones in spring. Animals have different ways to survive through the winter. Some mammals, such as squirrels and hedgehogs, hibernate (go to sleep for months in a concealed place) when it is cold and food is scarce. Animals that remain active during the winter, even if they have extra fat and fur, still need food to survive. Many birds migrate to warmer climates; those that do not benefit from people putting out food for them. You may hang a nut feeder from a tree near the school.

Use the activity to talk about the community of animals and plants living in the wood, and how they are dependent on each other. The animals survive by eating plants or other animals, so building up a food chain or a food web.

Answers

1. April to November.
2. 6 months.
3. Acorns. (Picture of an acorn.)
4. Autumn
5. There are no leaves on the trees, so more sunlight can reach the bluebells and primroses and help them to grow.
6. Two
7. April and May.
8. Rabbits mate and produce young rabbits for most of the year, so the rabbit population in the wood is kept high. They also feed on grass, which is available all year round.
9. Oak, ash, hazel, sweet chestnut, bluebell, primrose.
10. Grass, any other green woodland plant. (Not fungi.)
11. Examples may include:
grass -> rabbit -> fox
hazelnut -> squirrel -> owl
12. More food is available for the young owls. (Owls feed mainly on voles and mice, which are not featured in the chart.)

What will I find in the wood?

Mrs Thompson took her Year 6 class on a walk through a wood near the school in the spring. They saw that bluebells and primroses were growing close to the trees. They saw some catkins growing on hazel bushes, and some squirrels and rabbits scurrying around.

John, Amy and Sophie used books, the Internet and CD-ROMs to find out about some of the plants and animals that live in oak woodland, and the changes they would see over a year.

	Jan	Feb	Mar	Apr	May	Jun	Jul	Aug	Sep	Oct	Nov	Dec
Oak				F	F				Acorns	Acorns		
Ash				F	F					Ash keys	Ash keys	
Hazel	F	F	F	F					Nuts	Nuts		
Sweet chestnut				F	F				Nuts	Nuts		
Bluebell				F	F							
Primrose		F	F	F	F							
Squirrel		M	M	M			M	M				
Rabbit		M	M	M	M	M	M	M	M	M		
Fox	M	M										
Owl				M								

Key

F – in flower or catkin   M – mating season   ▦ – in leaf/producing babies

Questions

1. In which months does the oak tree have leaves?

2. For how many months does the ash tree have leaves?

3. What fruit is produced by the oak tree? Draw a picture of the fruit.

4. In which season of the year are nuts produced?

5. Bluebells and primroses grow in the soil close to the trees. Why is February to March a good time for them to grow leaves and then produce flowers?

6. How many times in each year are litters of young squirrels produced?

7. When do foxes produce their young?

8. Why are there always so many rabbits in the wood?

9. Which of the living things listed in the table are producers?

10. Name two other producers that you might find in a wood.

11. One example of a food chain is:

chestnut ⟹ squirrel ⟹ owl

Give two more examples of food chains using the living things in the wood.

12. Why do you think owls rear their young in the summer?

INVESTIGATING BONE SIZES

National Curriculum Science KS2 PoS Sc2: 1a, 1c, 2e
QCA Science Unit 6A: Interdependence and adaptation
Scottish 5–14 Guidelines Science Variety and characteristic features – Level C

HOW TO GATHER THE DATA

This activity can be used as part of a sequence of activities exploring variation within and between species. If each child in the class measures the length of another child's bone (the humerus or upper arm bone is easier than the thigh bone), the data can be collated and some idea of the variation in bone size within the population can be gained. Data such as those used to provide the graph, which shows the variation in bone sizes within the mammal group, are not easy to obtain, but most natural history museums have a series of skulls which can be used to show variation. The Natural History Museum in London (www.nhm.ac.uk) has activities based on bone sizes as part of its *Investigate* workshops; classes can be booked in to take part. Comparative data on the size of bones in the human, the gorilla and the baboon can be obtained from www.eskeletons.org, but the bones would need to be carefully selected for meaningful patterns to be clear in the data.

THE SCIENCE BEHIND THE DATA

This activity uses a scatter graph to show that there is a general trend for the thigh bone to become longer as the animal becomes longer. However, there is great variety between related species (for example, domestic cats and tigers), and even within species (for example, the Basset Hound and the Great Dane are both dogs but of different sizes). Selective breeding of dogs and horses has produced a great variety of shapes and sizes. Showing the children pictures and creating a display will make the data more meaningful for them.

If the graph is drawn showing only the faster-moving animals, there is much greater correlation between the length of the thigh bone and the length of the animal. Faster-moving animals have long, slender leg bones in relation to their body size. Human bones vary in size and shape from one person to another, but most of the variations are small. Tall people tend to have longer bones than shorter people, particularly leg bones – the thigh bone makes up $1/5$ to $1/4$ of the body's height.

The diameter of a bone is also linked to the size and weight of the animal (pictures from Dorling Kindersley's *Eyewitness Guide to the Skeleton* will show this). The femur often has a particularly large diameter to carry the animal's mass and allow efficient propulsion of the legs.

Answers
1. Giraffe.
2. Yes, the giraffe has the longest thigh bone.
3. The point for the giraffe is the highest and the furthest to the right.
4. 52cm
5. 20cm
6. 28cm
7. The longer the animal, the longer the thigh bone.
8. Mammals
9. The seal
10. The seal can live both in water and on land; all the other mammals shown in the graph live on land. The seal is adapted to live in water: its femurs (thigh bones) are unusually short for a mammal, because they are placed inside the body to give a streamlined shape. Seals swim using their back flippers, which contain its shin and foot bones.

Investigating bone sizes

A group of children found some data about bone sizes in various reference sources. They decided to see whether there was a pattern that longer animals had longer bones.

length of animal

The children plotted the length of the thigh bone against the body length of the animal (see illustration) to give a scatter graph.

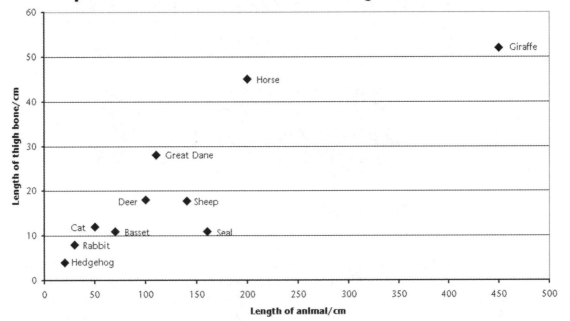

Comparison of size of animal with size of thigh bone

Questions

1. Which is the longest animal?

2. Does the longest animal have the longest thigh bone?

3. Explain how you decided this.

4. How long is the thigh bone of the longest animal?

5. What is the body length of the shortest animal?

6. How long is the thigh bone of the Great Dane?

7. What can you say about the general relationship between the length of the thigh bone and the length of the animal?

8. To which group of vertebrates do all these animals belong?

9. Which animal fits the pattern least well?

10. Why do you think that is? Look at some pictures and think about the animal's habitat if you need some help to decide.

HANDLING SCIENCE DATA YEAR 6

COMPOST HEAP

National Curriculum Science KS2 PoS Sc2: 5f
QCA Science Unit 6B: Micro-organisms
Scottish 5–14 Guidelines Science Variety and characteristic features – Levels E, F

HOW TO GATHER THE DATA

This investigation can be carried out using a 2-litre plastic bottle (see diagram). Use fresh grass cuttings rather than general waste: they don't smell as bad! Datalogging is a good method for this activity, since you can set up one investigation and leave it running all week ('continuous logging'), then download all the data at a later date. Alternatively, groups of children can set up their own compost heaps and use one set of datalogging sensors to take readings in turn each day or half-day ('snapshot logging').

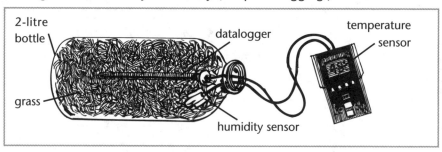

THE SCIENCE BEHIND THE DATA

The mechanism of a compost heap is very complex, as any gardener will tell you. Insects and other small animals will crawl or fly into the plant material, and the micro-organisms that are found everywhere on living material will multiply there. These organisms evolve an ecosystem in which they all benefit from each other. The temperature and humidity increase because respiration by all the living organisms is taking place. They release enzymes that break down the large cellulose molecules in vegetable matter into smaller molecules, which combine with oxygen to provide energy for all the metabolic processes in their cells. Carbon dioxide, water and energy are all products of respiration. The fact that the temperature increases without any outside source of heat being applied means that a chemical reaction (in this case, respiration) must be taking place.

The two graphs have a similar shape, which is significant: it shows that the same process (respiration) is affecting both factors. The two graphs cross, but this is not significant in scientific terms: it just happens because they have different units (on the same number scale). The respiration processes take some time to reach a significant level (as the population of micro-organisms starts to rise), so there is a 'lag time' at the beginning. The processes release energy (so the temperature rises) and water (so the humidity increases). They both increase at a steady rate until they reach a maximum level at which the rate of production of heat and water are equal to the rate at which they are escaping from the compost heap, so the temperature and humidity stay constant. If new vegetable matter is added, this rate of decay can be maintained indefinitely. The decayed material can be used as fertiliser to provide nutrients for plants in the soil.

Answers
1. 15°C
2. 55%
3. It stayed constant.
4. It increased.
5. It stayed constant.
6. 48°C
7. The temperature had levelled out at a maximum (rate of heat gain = rate of heat loss).
8. Living things were feeding on the compost and releasing heat.
9. Yes – children's own answer.
10. The shapes of the two graphs are very similar. (See 'The science behind the data' above.)

Compost heap

Ryan, Anthony and Lauren set up a compost heap of grass cuttings, old leaves and waste vegetables in a container. They monitored the temperature and humidity for 80 hours (about $3\frac{1}{2}$ days) using a datalogger.

This is a graph of their results.

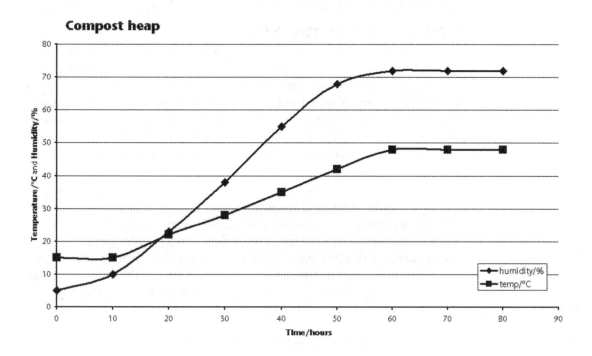

Questions

1. What was the temperature of the compost heap at the start of the investigation?

2. What was the humidity after 40 hours?

3. What happened to the temperature in the first 10 hours?

4. What happened to the humidity of the compost heap between 10 hours and 60 hours?

5. What happened to the temperature of the compost heap between 60 hours and 80 hours?

6. What do you think the temperature would be after 90 hours (if the conditions stayed the same)?

7. Explain your answer to Question 6.

8. Why did the temperature of the compost heap rise during the investigation?

9. Do you think the rise in temperature and the rise in humidity were caused by the same process?

10. Give a reason for your answer to Question 9.

HANDLING SCIENCE DATA YEAR 6

ADDING YEAST TO FLOUR

> ***National Curriculum Science*** KS2 PoS Sc2: 5f
> ***QCA Science*** Unit 6B: Micro-organisms
> ***Scottish 5–14 Guidelines Science*** Variety and characteristic features – Level F

HOW TO GATHER THE DATA

You will need to carry out some exploratory work to find the best conditions for this investigation. Fresh yeast can be used, but dried yeast is more readily available, and can be stored and weighed easily. In our investigation, 20g of plain flour was mixed with 1g of sugar, 2g of dried yeast and 25cm³ of water at 40°C. (Warm water activates the dried yeast – water at room temperature has very little effect.) Alternatively, you can make a solution of dried yeast and warm water and leave it for 10 minutes to activate before adding it to the flour.

Mix the water with the dry ingredients to make a sticky dough. Adding this to a 250cm³ measuring cylinder without it sticking to the sides requires patience and great skill, and most children will probably find it frustrating. To make it easier, you can pour the sticky dough into a powder funnel placed in the measuring cylinder – the dough should drop to the bottom. The children can then observe the initial volume and how it changes with time. (Powder funnels can be obtained from CAMLAB, Norman Way Industrial Estate, Cambridge, CB4 5QE; tel 01954 233100.)

THE SCIENCE BEHIND THE DATA

This activity should be done as part of a cross-curricular science/design and technology topic on making bread. It covers two QCA science units for Year 6: yeast is a useful micro-organism (a fungus), and fermenting dough is an irreversible change. Emphasise that yeast is a living thing: it needs food (and warmth) to grow. It feeds on the sugars present in flour (and the added sugar).

Ask the children to make unleavened bread by mixing flour and water, then baking the mixture – the appearance and taste can be compared to ordinary bread. Modern bread is usually made from flour, water, salt (for flavour) and yeast. It has a honeycomb structure: a solid foam with pockets of carbon dioxide spread evenly through it. Sugars in the flour are broken down into smaller glucose units and then fermented by enzymes (chemically active molecules) in the yeast. Alcohol and carbon dioxide are formed, and the carbon dioxide aerates the dough.

When the flour is kneaded with water to make dough, the proteins in the flour form an elastic material called gluten. When the dough ferments, it stretches and traps the carbon dioxide. When the dough is baked, the carbon dioxide expands, the alcohol evaporates, and the starch and gluten harden to provide a rigid shape.

Answers
1. About 24cm³.
2. 78cm³
3. 22°C
4. 5°C
5. Answers around 90cm³.
6. 37°C
7. The higher the temperature, the faster the volume of the dough increases. (If the temperature were too high, the yeast would be killed off. For comments on comparative statements, see page 6 in the Introduction.)
8. Yeast
9. A gas was being produced. (The child may predict that the gas is carbon dioxide. If the child says it is 'air', relate the process to human respiration.)
10. No. The change in the dough is a chemical change, and so irreversible.
11. Yeast is a living organism, so it needs warmth to grow and carry out respiration (producing carbon dioxide).

Adding yeast to flour

Simon, Neal and Jenny were making dough for a pizza base. They added yeast to a mixture of flour, salt and margarine. They kneaded the dough and left it in a warm place. Later, they noticed that it had doubled in size. They discussed this with their teacher and decided to investigate what was happening.

They mixed dried yeast, flour, sugar and warm water, put the dough into a measuring cylinder and recorded how the volume of the mixture changed with time. They did this at three different temperatures: in the fridge (5°C), at room temperature (22°C) and near a radiator (37°C). They also used a control sample with no yeast (at room temperature).

They recorded their results on this graph.

The children observed that bubbles appeared at the top of the sticky dough in the measuring cylinder, and that a smell like fresh bread was produced.

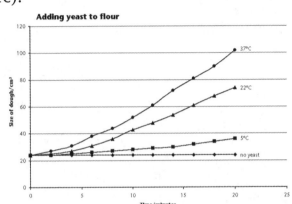

Adding yeast to flour

Questions

1. What was the volume of each dough sample at the start of the investigation?

2. By how much did the volume of the dough with yeast change in 20 minutes when it was left at 37°C?

3. At which temperature did the volume of the dough change by 50cm³ in 20 minutes?

4. At which temperature did the volume of the dough change very little?

5. What do you predict would be the final volume of the dough at room temperature (22°C) if it were left for 25 minutes?

6. If you were making bread or a pizza base, which would be the best temperature at which to leave your dough to rise?

7. How does the temperature of the dough affect the change in volume?

8. What material present in the mixture was making the dough expand?

9. What do you think was making the dough change its volume? (Hint: think about other things that change in volume, such as a balloon.)

10. Do you think it is possible for the dough to go back to its original size? Explain your answer.

11. Why do you think yeast works better in warm conditions?

TRAVELLING TO SCHOOL

> *National Curriculum Science* KS2 PoS Sc1: 1a; Sc2: 2h, 5a
> *QCA Science* Unit 5G/6H: Enquiry in environmental and technological contexts
> *Scottish 5–14 Guidelines Science* Interaction of living things with their environment – Level D; Social health – Level D

Answers

1. 64%
2. 53%
3. A 12% decrease (64% – 53%).
4. 25%
5. 38%
6. A 13% increase (38% – 25%).
7. More children travelled to school by car, and fewer children walked to school, in 1999 than in 1985.
8. Yes
9. The number of secondary school children travelling by bicycle to school went down from 6% in 1985 to 3% in 1999.
10. It is not safe for young children to cycle on the roads.
11. Secondary schools are usually further away from where the children live.
12. Yes, because more of the children walked to school.
13. Exercise is good for health, because the muscles are stronger and the heart and lungs work better if exercise is taken regularly.
14. Discuss the reasons with the children. Because there are more cars, it is more dangerous for children to cross roads than it was 14 years ago. Other reasons might include lack of parent time, both parents driving to work (dropping off children on the way) and so on.
15. Exhaust fumes from the car get into the atmosphere. They cause people to have difficulty breathing, and may cause asthma attacks. Ask the children whether they have smelled fumes from car exhausts when a car is being filled up with petrol.

HOW TO GATHER THE DATA

The data for this activity can easily be downloaded from the Department for Transport, Local Government and the Regions website (main site www.dtlr.gov.uk or statistics www.transtat.dft.gov.uk). Other data are available from this site that children could investigate. It would be easy to carry out a survey in your class or your school to find out how the children travel to school, comparing the results with the national data. Using data such as these allows children to acquire the process skills required under the 'Considering evidence and evaluating' strand of Sc1 (Scientific enquiry).

THE SCIENCE BEHIND THE DATA

The issue of how children travel to school is an important one, and it demonstrates the links between science and social issues. You can use this theme to discuss the relationship between scientific and technological advances, such as the production of cheaper and more efficient cars, and their effects on the environment and our health. Fewer primary school children walk to school now than a decade ago. There are many reasons for this: the pressures of modern lifestyles, safety issues regarding children crossing roads on their own, lack of additional family members (such as grandparents) in the neighbourhood. More secondary children travel on the bus and fewer walk to school than primary children, because the secondary school is usually further away. Walking to school is good exercise for the leg muscles, heart and lungs. Children generally take less exercise these days than in the past, which is a major concern for the health of society.

Using cars for short journeys is bad for the environment, particularly in cities. Pollutants from car exhausts, such as the gases nitrogen dioxide and carbon monoxide, as well as particulates, unburnt hydrocarbon and benzene from petrol, are all bad for our health. Nitrogen dioxide and low-level ozone formed from the reaction of nitrogen dioxide with sunlight cause respiratory problems. Carbon monoxide is poisonous, and benzene is a carcinogen. The number of asthma cases in the UK is increasing, and there is no doubt that air pollution contributes to this problem. On short journeys, such as those from home to school, catalytic converters in cars (which convert the toxic gases to less harmful ones) are less effective because they have not reached optimum temperature (statistics from the DTLR website show that 80% of journeys to school are less than 2 miles).

Travelling to school

Mrs Jones found out how many children in her Year 6 class walked to school, how many cycled and how many came by car. The school was situated in a medium-sized village where most of the families lived close to the school, so most of the children walked.

Then she found out what the national statistics were for children travelling to school:

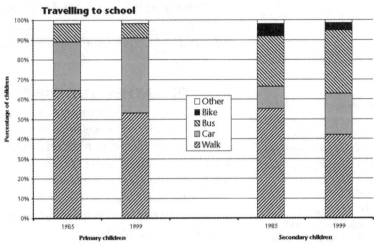

Questions

1. What percentage of primary children walked to school in 1985?

2. What percentage of primary children walked to school in 1999?

3. What is the difference between the two, and is it an increase or a decrease?

4. What percentage of primary children travelled to school by car in 1985?

5. What percentage of primary children travelled to school by car in 1999?

6. What is the difference between the two, and is it an increase or a decrease?

7. What can you say about the changes in how primary children travelled to school between 1985 and 1999?

8. Look at the right-hand part of the graph. Is the pattern the same for secondary children?

9. What happened to the number of secondary children who travelled to school by bicycle in the years between 1985 and 1999?

10. Why do primary children not ride bicycles to school?

11. Why do more secondary children travel to school by bus than primary children?

12. Do you think children were fitter in 1985 than in 1999? Explain your answer.

13. Why is it a good idea to take exercise by walking or cycling to school?

14. Why do you think the ways in which children of all ages travel to school have changed in the last 14 years?

15. Many car journeys cover short distances, such as a journey to school. Cars pollute the environment. Can you explain how?

WHAT'S IN THE DUSTBIN?

National Curriculum Science KS2 PoS Sc2: 5a
QCA Science Unit 5G/6H: Enquiry in environmental and technological contexts
Scottish 5–14 Guidelines Science Interaction of living things with their environment – Level D

HOW TO GATHER THE DATA

This activity shows how secondary data can be used effectively in science to support the children's ideas or investigations. The data shown opposite can be obtained from local councils, many of whom keep quite extensive statistics about waste disposal. Data showing the amount of material collected and recycled should also be available.

In Chester (see www.chestercc.gov.uk – index r for recycling), households place different materials in separate coloured plastic bags, which are collected every two weeks: plastics, aluminium cans, paper and card, and textiles. A brown wheelie bin is provided for garden waste. Large banks are provided for collecting glass, paper and textiles. This kind of scheme is now run by many local authorities.

THE SCIENCE BEHIND THE DATA

This activity provides children with the opportunity to reflect on the amount of rubbish that they and the rest of society generate. You can show them the rubbish that is collected within the school in one day, or send them (wearing gloves or carrying litter pickers) on a litter pick around the school playground.

Our society uses too much packaging and does not recycle enough. Ask the children whether they know what happens to the waste from their dustbin. Ask them whether they have been to the nearest waste disposal site, and what sort of things are dumped there. Have they seen rubbish dumped in the countryside? Tell them where the nearest landfill site is, and what they would see there (rubbish and seagulls).

This important issue links well with work on citizenship. There are only a limited number of sites that can be used for landfill – sites near rivers, for example, are questionable due to the leaching of materials from the landfill into water courses. The current landfill sites are being filled up very quickly. An alternative is to burn rubbish using an incinerator – but most people do not want an incinerator near their home, as there are worries about toxic gases that may be emitted.

Future generations will need to recycle more. Britain lags behind the rest of Europe in recycling, and it is only by educating our children that we can pave the way for change. Ask the children what materials can be recycled. Make a list of recyclable materials, from aluminium cans to vegetable waste, and highlight the benefits of recycling. Valuable information and resources to do with recycling can be obtained from www.tecweb.com/recycle/school.htm. This is a part of www.tecweb.org, which belongs to the Education Coalition.

Answers
1. Paper and card.
2. It could be taken to the bottle banks provided at community centres and supermarkets for recycling glass.
3. Packaging
4. Vegetable matter/garden waste.
5. Make a compost heap if possible, or use a separate bin for vegetable matter.
6. Bacteria and tiny animals will break down the vegetable matter, which will decay to make compost. The compost can be added to soil as a source of humus, which will help plants to grow.
7a. Paper and card can be taken to a paper skip.
b. Glass can be disposed of in bottle banks.
c. Plastics can be put into special collecting bags provided by the council, or taken to special containers for disposal.
d. Vegetable waste can be put on a compost heap.
e. Textiles can be recycled through charity shops or containers used to supply materials for overseas aid.
f. Aluminium cans can be recycled in bags or other containers provided by the council.
8. If these materials are dumped on landfill sites, they will contaminate the local environment. Recycling also helps to conserve the world's resources.

What's in the dustbin?

A class of primary school children were discussing recycling. Their teacher obtained some data from the local council that showed the contents of an average dustbin.

The children presented the data in the form of a pie chart:

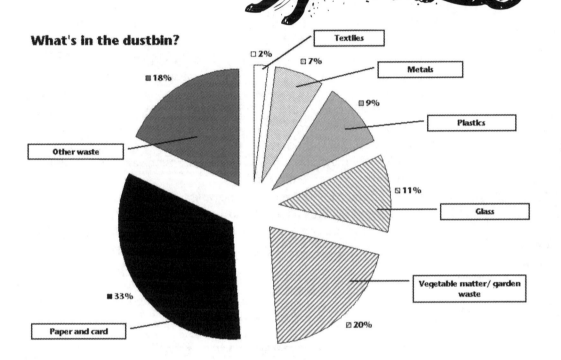

What's in the dustbin?

- 2%
- Textiles 7%
- Metals 9%
- Plastics 11%
- Glass
- Vegetable matter/ garden waste 20%
- Paper and card 33%
- Other waste 18%

Questions

1. Which material was the most common type of waste found in the dustbin?

2. Where could people take glass instead of putting it in the dustbin?

3. Where do you think most of the plastic waste comes from?

4. Which material was the second most common type of waste found in the dustbin?

5. What should people do with this waste material instead of putting it in the dustbin?

6. How would that lead to the waste material being reused?

7. What should we do with the following materials instead of dumping them in the dustbin? **a)** Paper and card. **b)** Glass. **c)** Plastics. **d)** Vegetable waste. **e)** Textiles. **f)** Aluminium cans.

8. Give two general reasons why we should do those things.

HANDLING SCIENCE DATA YEAR 6

DISSOLVING WHITE CRYSTALS

National Curriculum Science KS2 PoS Sc3: 2a, d; 3b, d
QCA Science Unit 6C: More about dissolving
Scottish 5–14 Guidelines Science Changing materials – Level C

HOW TO GATHER THE DATA

All the materials can be obtained from a chemist or your local secondary school, and are safe to use in the primary school. Calcium carbonate is also called chalk, but it is not the chalk used in school. The simplest way of carrying out this investigation is for the children to work in groups, with each group investigating a different material. Each group should put 100cm³ of water at room temperature into a beaker. They should weigh out 10g of the solid (or 20g of sugar or citric acid), add it to the beaker and stir until it dissolves. (Using more of the more soluble solids is appropriate, because the amount that will dissolve is the variable being tested.) If there is still solid left at the bottom, no more will dissolve. Measuring solubility to the nearest 10g is suitable for this age group. The figures in the activity are for comparison purposes only; they may differ from scientific data, since accurate solubilities are measured in a different way.

You could select three of the powders (say citric acid, alum and baking soda) and ask the children to find out which is which. They can identify citric acid from the solubility data. If they mix it with baking powder in water, fizzing will occur (producing carbon dioxide). Mixing citric acid with alum will have no effect. Use a story to arouse interest, such as: *I want to make a cake, but I've dropped all the containers of white powder from my kitchen cupboard into the sink and the labels have fallen off. Can you help me find the baking powder?*

THE SCIENCE BEHIND THE DATA

Solids dissolve by this process: first the solute (solid) particles separate; then the solvent (liquid) particles move apart to make room for the solute particles; then the solvent particles surround the solute particles. Heat is absorbed in steps 1 and 2, then heat is released in step 3. If the heat changes do not balance, there will be a temperature change.

The energy change during dissolving depends on the solute. Sugar (sucrose) and citric acid are both covalently bonded solids: the forces holding the solid together are less strong than the forces holding ionically bonded solids (the other four materials tested) together. More energy is needed to separate and dissolve ionic solids. The forces holding calcium carbonate together are so strong that water cannot break down the solid, so it is insoluble.

When no more solid will dissolve, the solution is said to be saturated. When a solution evaporates, solid crystals can be reformed.

Answers
1. Sugar.
2. Calcium carbonate. It is insoluble.
3. 180g
4. Alum, baking powder.
5. 40g
6. 140g
7. 250g. (Children may suggest 100g, 150g or other values. Demonstrate the correct answer, using scales. Ask the children to explain this result.)
8. Leave a small amount of the solution in a shallow dish to evaporate.
9. As for Question 8 – but leave the solution in a cool place so it will evaporate slowly.
10. Same amount of water, same number of stirs, same rate of stirring, same temperature, same amount of time.
11. The main features are these. Measure 100cm³ of water into a container. Add 10g of the white crystals. Stir the mixture a fixed number of times. See whether all the solid dissolves. If it does, add another 10g and stir. Repeat until no more will dissolve.

Dissolving white crystals

Suki, Aftab and Hannah had been given some white crystalline materials by their teacher. These all had different names: salt, sugar, calcium carbonate, baking powder, citric acid and alum. The children decided to find out how much of each material dissolved in 100cm³ of water at room temperature (20°C).

They recorded their results as a bar chart.
(The amount of material is given to the nearest 10g.)

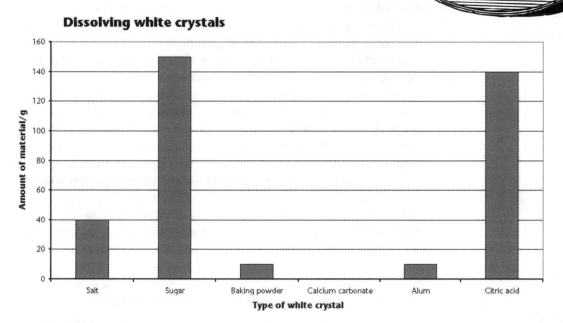

Questions

1. Which material is the most soluble in water?

2. Which material does not dissolve in water? What word describes this property?

3. How much sugar dissolved in 100cm³ of water at room temperature?

4. Of the materials that did dissolve, which were the least soluble?

5. How much salt dissolved in 100cm³ of water at room temperature?

6. How much more sugar than salt dissolved in the water?

7. If 150g of sugar is dissolved in 100cm³ of water, what will be the mass of the solution?

8. How would you obtain the original solids from their solutions in water?

9. What would be the best way to make large crystals?

10. What should the children have kept the same to make their test fair?

11. Write a set of instructions that will tell someone else how to carry out the investigation.

HANDLING SCIENCE DATA YEAR 6

SUGAR IN HOT TEA

National Curriculum Science KS2 PoS Sc3: 2a, c, d
QCA Science Unit 6C: More about dissolving
Scottish 5–14 Guidelines Science Changing materials – Level E

HOW TO GATHER THE DATA

This is a good activity for developing higher-order investigation skills. If all the groups of children carry out the first measurement (the time for 10g of sugar to dissolve at room temperature), you can collect the times from all the groups and discuss why these are different. They may suggest a number of reasons, but the most important one is that it is difficult (even for an experienced scientist) to observe exactly when the last grains of sugar have disappeared. You can then ask them how to obtain a more reliable result. Each group can take three measurements and calculate the average.

Divide the children into groups, each measuring the dissolving time for 10g of sugar at a different temperature. The group working with water at 10°C may need to have it cooled in the fridge. Safety warnings regarding the use of hot water should be given. We suggest that you demonstrate the test using water at 60°C. It is important that each group adds the sugar and then stirs quickly to dissolve it, so the temperature of the water does not change too much during the investigation.

Use this investigation to discuss the nature of scientific evidence. If the results from all the groups are plotted, it is unlikely that the points will all fall on a 'perfect' line. Introduce the idea of drawing a line of best fit (in this case, a curve).

Answers

1. 19 seconds
2. 80 seconds
3. 47°C
4. 10–15 seconds
5. 81 seconds
6. Because of the difficulty of measuring the time taken for the sugar to dissolve. Repeating the timing three times and calculating the mean time would help to reduce these errors.
7. The higher the temperature, the faster the sugar dissolves. (See the Introduction, page 6, for notes on comparative statements.)
8. Stirring, using a greater volume of water, using finer particles of sugar (for example, icing sugar).
9. The amount of water, the mass of sugar, the rate of stirring, the type of sugar.
10. As the temperature increases, the sugar particles and water particles move faster, so there is more energy to break down the crystals. The sugar particles fit more easily into the spaces between the water particles, and the time taken for the sugar to dissolve decreases.

THE SCIENCE BEHIND THE DATA

Most children know that materials dissolve more quickly and completely in hot water than in cold water. This is the source of the common confusion between melting and dissolving, since they perceive that dissolving needs heat. You can use the QCA unit 'More about dissolving' to address this distinction. In melting, only one material is involved (for example, ice melts to water). In dissolving, two materials are involved: the solute (normally a solid such as sugar) and a solvent (such as water). They combine to form a solution. You can emphasise this by weighing the solution to show that the solute is still there, and by leaving a small amount of solution to evaporate.

Dissolving has three steps (in particle terms). The solute particles separate from each other; then the solvent particles move apart to make room for the solute particles; then the solvent particles surround the solute particles. More energy is available at higher temperatures, so all the particles move faster and the solute dissolves more quickly.

Sugar in hot tea

Ben, Josh and Clemmy were talking about drinking tea. They all stirred sugar into their tea – and thought it must dissolve well in the hot tea, as they had not seen any sugar left at the bottom of the cup. They decided to find out whether sugar dissolves faster in hot water than in cold water.

They plotted their results as a line graph:

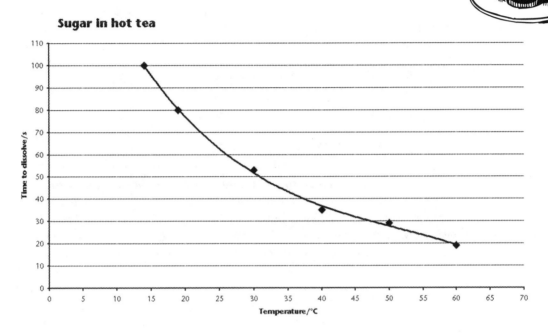

Questions

1. How long did it take the sugar to dissolve at 60°C?

2. How long did it take the sugar to dissolve at room temperature (19°C)?

3. If it took the sugar 30 seconds to dissolve, what would the temperature be?

4. How long do you think it would take for the sugar to dissolve at 70°C?

5. How much longer did it take the sugar to dissolve at 14°C than at 60°C?

6. Why don't all the points fall exactly on the curved line? What could be done to improve the fit of the points to the line?

7. How does the temperature affect the time taken for the sugar to dissolve?

8. What other factors, apart from temperature, help sugar to dissolve more easily?

9. What factors should the children have kept the same to make their experiment a fair test?

10. Why do you think sugar dissolves faster at higher temperatures?

BURNING CANDLES

National Curriculum Science KS2 PoS Sc3: 2f, g
QCA Science Unit 6D: Reversible and irreversible changes
Scottish 5–14 Guidelines Science Changing materials – Level D

HOW TO GATHER THE DATA

This simple investigation can be set up in a safe place and monitored while the children do other activities related to this topic. It is necessary to use an accurate balance to carry out this investigation. Balances that weigh to the nearest 0.1g can be obtained for use in primary schools for about £50 to £80 (shop around!), and are a good investment. Alternatively, they can be borrowed from a friendly secondary school. Put a dish on the balance to protect it from molten wax (and to make sure that the molten wax is not lost).

THE SCIENCE BEHIND THE DATA

Candles burn remarkably evenly. At one time they were used as clocks, with regularly spaced rings marked around them at appropriate heights to measure the hours. The wax is a hydrocarbon (a substance made up of hydrogen and carbon combined). When it burns, it combines with oxygen to form water vapour and carbon dioxide, which are given off as gases. This is why the mass decreases. A small amount of carbon from the burning wax is released as floating solid particles (smoke). The wick burns as well, and gives the same products. You can easily demonstrate the formation of water by putting a glass jar over a lighted candle: condensation will form on the inside of the jar. If you do this, the candle will soon go out, indicating that the oxygen inside the glass jar is being used up.

The formation of new materials is the best definition and the best evidence indicator for the children to use in classifying a change as non-reversible (or irreversible). In the context of a chemical reaction, an irreversible change is one in which the new materials made cannot be changed back into the original materials.

Ask the children what is happening when the candle burns: *Where is the wax going? What is happening to it?* This can be very enlightening. Many children think the wax is all still there: it has just melted and run into the dish. However, if you carry on burning the candle for long enough and make sure it is vertical, there won't be any wax left in the dish – so that idea is not supported by the evidence.

Answers

1. (Diagram of a burning candle on a dish or tile, placed on a balance.)
2. 11.2g
3. 5.7g
4. The mass decreased steadily.
5. The candle wax was burning away (forming smoke, as well as invisible carbon dioxide and water vapour).
6. It was burning at the same rate all the time.
7. The graph is a straight line, indicating that the candle lost the same amount of mass in each ten-minute period.
8. 0g
9. The trend of the graph indicates that the mass will be 0g at that time: all the wax will have burned away. (The child may respond from experience that some unburned wax is always left, so there will be a small mass. Relate the answers to Question 8.)
10. Non-reversible (or irreversible).
11. New materials are being made. (This is the best definition to use, since it always applies. Discourage answers such as 'It cannot change back' – for example, if you break a stick it cannot change back, but no new materials have been made.)

Burning candles

In this activity, Mrs Taylor put a candle on an electronic balance. Then she lit the candle and started a clock at the same time.

This graph shows how the mass of the candle changed with time.

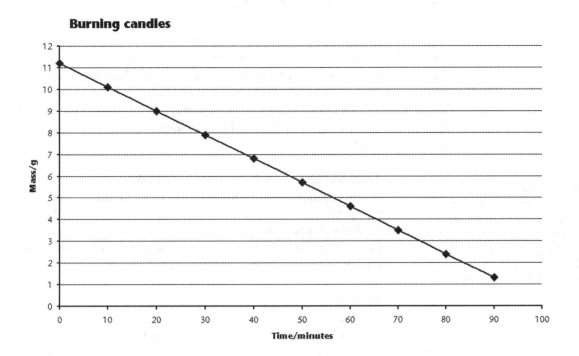

Questions

1. Draw a diagram to show the experiment.

2. What was the mass of the candle at the start of the experiment?

3. What was the mass of the candle after 50 minutes?

4. What was happening to the mass of the candle as time went on?

5. Use your scientific knowledge to explain why this happened.

6. Do you think the candle was burning faster at any time, or was it burning at the same rate all the time?

7. How did the graph help you to answer Question 6?

8. What do you think the mass of the candle was at 100 minutes (if the conditions stayed the same)?

9. Explain your answer to Question 8.

10. Is the candle burning a reversible change or a non-reversible change?

11. Give a reason for your answer to Question 10.

HANDLING SCIENCE DATA YEAR 6

ALKA SELTZER

National Curriculum Science KS2 PoS Sc3: 2a, f
QCA Science Unit 6D: Reversible and irreversible changes
Scottish 5–14 Guidelines Science Changing materials – Level C

HOW TO GATHER THE DATA

It is necessary to use an accurate balance for this investigation. Balances that weigh to the nearest 0.1g can be obtained for use in primary schools for about £50 to £80 (shop around!), and are a good investment. Alternatively, they can be borrowed from a friendly secondary school. Put the container full of water on the balance and reset it to zero (most balances will do this). When you put the tablets in the water, you are immediately measuring the mass of the tablets. Most versions of these tablets contain paracetamol, so you will need to work safely.

THE SCIENCE BEHIND THE DATA

This is an example of a non-reversible or irreversible change. The formation of new materials is the best definition, and the best evidence indicator, for the children to use in classifying a change as reversible or irreversible. In this example, a gas is produced. The children can see the bubbles and understand that this is a new substance or material. The tablets contain a mixture of substances, including a solid acid and a carbonate. These react together when mixed with water to form the gas carbon dioxide. You can also show the presence of a gas by putting a tablet into some water in a resealable sandwich bag and sealing the bag: the bag expands as the gas is released.

The mass of the tablets decreases because the gas escapes into the air, but it does not go down to zero because some of the material dissolves into the water. If you do this activity using a screw-top plastic jar and you are quick to screw on the lid, you will not lose any gas and the mass of the system will stay the same; this shows that everything that you had at the start of your reaction is still there at the end, even though it may have changed into something different. If you then release the lid, the gas hisses out under pressure and the mass of the system decreases. If you carry out a chemical reaction, weighing all the substances at the start, then collect and weigh all the products together at the end, the system will weigh the same at the end as at the start. This principle is called the conservation of mass.

Answers

1. A diagram to show two fizzing tablets in a glass of water on a balance.
2. 5.9g
3. 5.2g
4. The mass of the tablets decreases.
5. 10 seconds (or 20 seconds) and 30 seconds.
6. This is the steepest part of the curve, so the tablets are losing mass most quickly at this time. (Or an answer that uses numbers to compare different parts of the line graph.)
7.

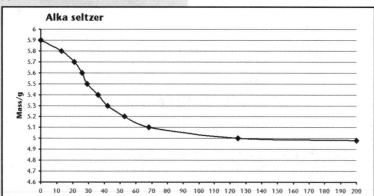

8. 11.8g
9. 1.8g
10. Two tablets lost 0.9g in 125 seconds, so four tablets will lose twice as much: 1.8g.
11. A non-reversible change.
12. The gas that was formed is a new substance or material.

Alka Seltzer

When you put Alka Seltzer tablets in a glass of water, they fizz and lots of bubbles suddenly appear in the glass. In this activity, we put a glass of water on a balance and set it to read zero. We dropped two tablets in the water and started the clock at the same time.

This graph shows how the mass changed with time.

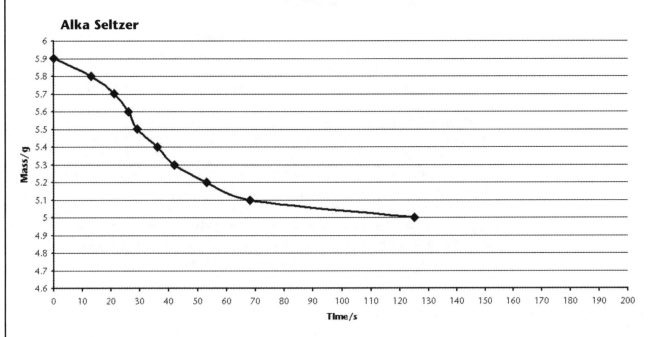

Questions

1. Draw a diagram to show what happened in this activity.

2. What was the mass of the two Alka Seltzer tablets at the start of the experiment?

3. What was the mass of the tablets after 50 seconds?

4. What happened to the mass of the tablets as the experiment went on?

5. Complete this sentence: The tablet was fizzing the most between ___ seconds and ___ seconds.

6. Explain your answer to Question 5.

7. Complete the line to show the mass up to 200 seconds (if the conditions stay the same).

8. What would be the mass at the start of the investigation if we used four tablets?

9. How much mass would the four tablets lose in 125 seconds?

10. Explain how you worked this out.

11. Is this an example of a reversible change or a non-reversible change?

12. Give a reason for your answer to Question 11.

FIZZ-POP ROCKETS

> *National Curriculum Science* KS2 PoS Sc3: 2a, f
> *QCA Science* Unit 6D: Reversible and irreversible changes
> *Scottish 5–14 Guidelines Science* Changing materials – Level E

HOW TO GATHER THE DATA

Children really enjoy doing this investigation (see B Kibble, 2001, *Primary Science Review 70* pp11–12). They can work in groups to investigate different factors that affect the time taken for the rocket to explode, such as the volume of water or the amount of tablet used. They may also like to investigate the volume of gas generated, using a balloon placed over the open tub to catch the gas.

A small ball of Blu-Tack pressed onto the underside of the lid will anchor the tablet. Make sure the lid is fixed on firmly (it will make a crisp sound when it clips on) before the tub is inverted. For safety, make sure the children step back as soon as they have inverted the rocket. They will need accurate stopwatches to time the explosion.

Black plastic film tubs can be obtained free from most shops that develop photographs. The clip-on lid allows the container to be used as a mini-rocket. Fizzy soluble Vitamin C tablets or Alka Seltzer (indigestion) tablets can be used. It is best to use only a quarter or half of a tablet so the 'fizz-pop time' is not too short for measurement and comparison.

Answers

1. 55°C
2. 10 seconds
3. 28 seconds
4. 20°C
5. About 70 seconds.
6. About 7 seconds.
7. The volume of water, the size of the tub, the type of tub, the amount of tablet used.
8. The water mixes with the tablet and a gas (carbon dioxide) is produced. The gas cannot escape, so the pressure builds up until it blows off the lid and fires the container into the air.
9. The higher the temperature, the shorter the fizz-pop time.
10. The children can use the planning boards (photocopiable pages 63 and 64) to design an investigation such as: using different volumes of water, using different amounts of tablet, using different brands of tablet, finding out how much gas is produced under different conditions (by collecting it in a balloon).

THE SCIENCE BEHIND THE DATA

This activity provides children with a simple introduction to an irreversible chemical reaction. (It may be simple, but it's still rocket science!) The graph shows an inverse relationship: the higher the temperature of the water, the shorter the time taken for the reaction to occur. This is true of many chemical reactions that the children will investigate later in secondary school, such as the reaction of magnesium or calcium carbonate with acid. You will need to discuss the nature of the pattern shown in the graph with the children. For many simple reactions, a 10°C rise in temperature will approximately double the rate of reaction, producing an exponential curve. The results shown opposite nearly fit this pattern, but not quite: the time taken for the reaction is less at 15°C than might be predicted from the rest of the graph (perhaps because Alka Seltzer is designed to dissolve in cold water).

An Alka Seltzer tablet (which contains calcium bicarbonate) reacts with water to produce carbon dioxide gas. When this happens in a sealed container, the lid can be blown off by the increased pressure of gas.

Fizz-pop rockets

Lizzie, Laura, Davie and Hamish were doing a rocket investigation with Mr Kibble, who was visiting their classroom. They used Blu-Tack to fix a quarter Alka Seltzer tablet inside each lid of five small plastic film tubs. Then they put 10cm³ water inside each tub. The water in each tub was at a different temperature.

They put the lid back on, inverted the tub and timed how long it took for the 'rocket' to explode.

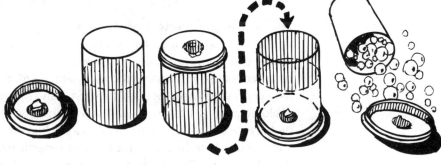

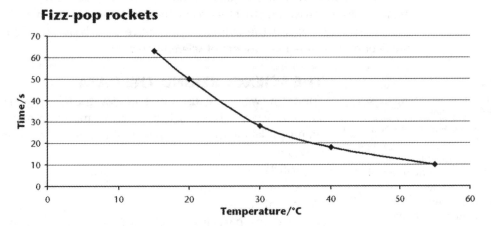

Fizz-pop rockets

Questions

1. At which temperature did the rocket explode the fastest?

2. How long did the rocket take to explode at that temperature?

3. How long did the rocket take to explode at 30°C?

4. At what temperature did it take 55 seconds to explode?

5. Using the graph, predict how long a rocket with water at 10°C would take to explode.

6. Using the graph, predict how long a rocket with water at 60°C would take to explode.

7. What factors did the children keep the same to make sure their tests were fair?

8. What happens when the tablet and the water mix?

9. What can you say about the relationship between the temperature and the fizz-pop time?

10. Think of another investigation that you could carry out using Alka Seltzer tablets, film tubs and water. Now plan out your investigation.

HANDLING SCIENCE DATA YEAR 6

WEIGHING WATER

> **National Curriculum Science** KS2 PoS Sc3: 2b, c, d
> **QCA Science** Unit 6D: reversible and irreversible changes
> **Scottish 5–14 Guidelines Science** Changing materials – Level C

HOW TO GATHER THE DATA

This is a simple investigation to carry out, but in order to obtain meaningful results you will need scales that weigh to the nearest 0.1g. These can be obtained for use in primary schools for about £50 to £80 (shop around!), and are a good investment for both the science and the maths curricula (this activity could be done just as well as part of a maths lesson). Alternatively, they could be borrowed from a friendly secondary school. You will obtain results over half an hour, and the children can do other activities while you are gathering data for this one. The children can also make predictions about what the next reading will be. You will find that they refine their predictions as the investigation proceeds: they will use the evidence they have as a basis for their new predictions, which is a key aspect of scientific thinking.

Answers

1. No. (Look for an explanation in the answer to Question 2.)

2. The evaporated water cannot get out with the lid over the dish, so the scales will still weigh the same amount of water, and the inside of the lid will have condensation on it. (Children may say that Jacki is right, because the evaporated water does not weigh anything. All responses need to be investigated further by gathering evidence.)

3. The mass decreased.

4. The water evaporated. Make sure the children explain this more fully: what happened to the water? (It is in the air, but we cannot see it: the particles are too small to see.)

5. The mass stayed the same.

6. The lid stopped the water particles from escaping into the air. The water particles stayed inside the dish, so they were still weighed.

7. a) 6g **b)** 1.5g **c)** About 0.2g (less than 0.5g).

8. The water cools down as it evaporates (one of the ways it loses heat is through evaporation). Then, as it cools down, it evaporates less quickly.

9. About 83g.

10. Yes

11. Eventually all the water would evaporate into the air, because more water particles would leave the water surface than would reach it from the air.

THE SCIENCE BEHIND THE DATA

The term 'weight' is used in everyday speech to mean the same as 'mass' – but in scientific terms, mass is measured in grams (or kilograms) whereas weight (a force) is measured in newtons.

Solids are held together by strong forces of attraction between the particles, which means that the particles do not move around: they only vibrate. In liquids, the

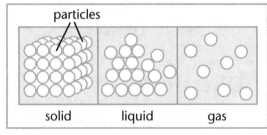

weaker forces between the particles allow them to move around within the boundaries of the liquid. The particles will move much more rapidly and move further apart if the liquid is heated.

If the particles are moving rapidly and they are near the surface, they can escape from the liquid altogether – a process known as evaporation. Evaporation will occur in a liquid at any temperature, but will occur more rapidly at higher temperatures. This is shown by the graph opposite: the slope of the graph decreases as the water cools. Since the particles that evaporate from the water surface have more energy than those that stay, evaporation causes the water to cool. The more it cools, the more slowly evaporation takes place – though it will continue indefinitely, unless there is so much humidity in the air that water particles return to the water surface as fast as they leave it. When the particles escape from the liquid, they are in a gaseous state: they are moving very rapidly, and are far apart.

Weighing water

Jacki and Jenny were investigating how water evaporates. One of the things they did was to put some very hot water in a dish and weigh the dish every five minutes.

"But what if we put a lid on the dish?" asked Jenny.

"I think it will still change in mass," said Jacki.

Questions

1. Do you agree with Jacki that the water will change in mass with the lid on?

2. Give a scientific explanation for your answer to Question 1.

They found out what happened with and without a lid on the dish, then plotted both sets of results on a graph.

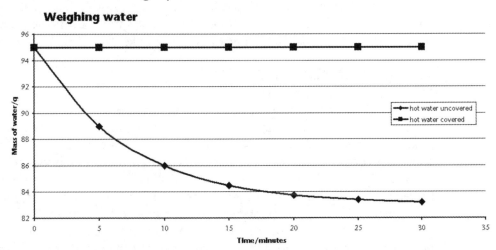

3. What happened to the mass of the water that was uncovered?

4. Explain scientifically why this happened.

5. What happened to the mass of the water that was covered?

6. Explain scientifically why this happened.

7. How much water was lost from the uncovered dish in **a)** 0–5 minutes, **b)** 10–15 minutes, **c)** 25–30 minutes?

8. Why do you think the mass of water lost every five minutes changes?

9. What do you think will be the mass of water in the uncovered dish after 35 minutes?

10. If the water were left long enough, would the mass of water in the uncovered dish fall to 0g?

11. Give a scientific explanation for your answer to Question 10.

MAKING TOAST

National Curriculum Science KS2 PoS Sc3: 2f, g
QCA Science Unit 6D Reversible and irreversible changes
Scottish 5–14 Guidelines Science Changing materials – Level D

HOW TO GATHER THE DATA

You can do a 'before and after' investigation such as this one easily, using an accurate balance. Balances that weigh to the nearest 0.1g can be obtained for use in primary schools for about £50 to £80 (shop around!), and are a good investment. Alternatively, they can be borrowed from a nearby secondary school.

Keep the children well back from the following demonstration. Put the slice of bread in the toaster and switch the toaster on. After 30s, eject the bread and weigh it quickly, then put it straight back in the toaster (with practice, you can do this in less than 10s). Then heat for another 30s, and so on. The toast will become very hot in the later stages, so you will need a glove to protect your fingers. You will also need to cover the scale pan so that the toast does not stain it (this is essential if you have borrowed the scales). If you carry out this investigation indoors, don't heat the toast as much as the account opposite describes: it will fill the classroom with smoke.

THE SCIENCE BEHIND THE DATA

Making toast is a familiar activity, but it is very fruitful in promoting children's discussion. They can work in pairs or groups to examine a slice of bread and use any common or scientific words to describe its properties. A class can produce as many as 30 different words to describe a slice of bread. They can then make predictions about what will happen to the bread in the toaster.

Bread is made from flour, water, fat and other ingredients. When it is heated in a toaster, the water evaporates. You can feel some dampness if you hold your hand above the top of the toaster (do not let the children do this). If you leave a slice of warm toast on the table, a damp patch will appear underneath, demonstrating that water comes out of the bread. In the later stages, when the smoke appears, the carbohydrate in the flour breaks down into water (which evaporates) and carbon or charcoal (the blackened material). You can write with this charcoal on a sheet of paper – children are often impressed by this.

An irreversible change, in the context of a chemical reaction, is best defined by saying that a new material or substance has been made rather than saying 'you cannot change it back'. The new materials in this case are the black charcoal and the smoke, made from the carbohydrate in the bread.

Answers

1. 0s to 30s.
2. 7 to 7½ minutes.
3. 9g
4. About 19g.
5. The water in the bread evaporated, and then some solid was lost as smoke. Give credit for any feasible responses.
6. No
7. There will be some burnt toast (charcoal) left.
8. The toast was burning.
9. An irreversible change.
10. Two new materials, charcoal and smoke, are produced.

Making toast

Mr Blackburn was doing a science lesson on reversible and irreversible changes in materials. He asked the class what would happen to a slice of bread when he put it in a toaster and switched the toaster on. Some children suggested that it would go hard, turn crispy, change colour, go smaller. Fiona suggested that it would go lighter. Mr Blackburn used some scales to measure the mass of the slice every 30 seconds it was being toasted.

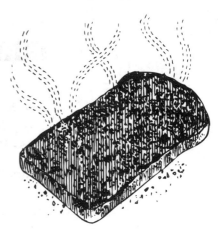

This is a graph of their results.

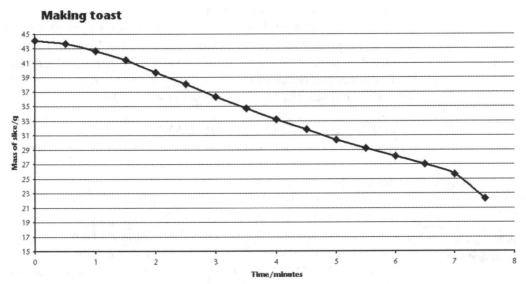

Questions

1. In which half-minute was there the smallest decrease in mass?

2. In which half-minute was there the largest decrease in mass?

3. How much mass was lost between 2 minutes and 5 minutes? Answer to the nearest 1g.

4. Predict the mass of the slice (to the nearest 1g) after 8 minutes in the toaster.

5. Why do you think the mass decreased?

6. Do you think the mass will go down to zero?

7. Explain your answer to Question 6.

8. At about 5 or 6 minutes, the bread started to smoke. By 7 minutes, lots of smoke came off it. What do you think was happening to the toast?

9. Was this a reversible change or an irreversible change?

10. Explain your answer to Question 9.

HANDLING SCIENCE DATA YEAR 6

IRREVERSIBLE CHANGES

National Curriculum Science KS2 PoS Sc3: 2a, f
QCA Science Unit 6D: Reversible and irreversible changes
Scottish 5–14 Guidelines Science Changing materials – Level C

HOW TO GATHER THE DATA

Irreversible changes can be a fascinating topic to teach, and children enjoy watching the chemical reactions. Make sure that all the children have a secure understanding of reversible changes such as melting, boiling, evaporating and dissolving (the latter two are quite difficult) before moving on to consider irreversible changes.

You can organise the children into groups to observe and measure the temperature changes occurring in a number of simple chemical reactions: citric acid with baking powder (sodium hydrogen carbonate), which is unusual because the temperature drops; citric acid with sodium carbonate (washing soda); white vinegar with sodium carbonate; plaster of Paris with water; and so on. Safety precautions need to be taken (see the ASE booklet *Be Safe!* or local authority guidelines for sensible advice): the children should wear safety spectacles (and face masks when handling plaster of Paris).

THE SCIENCE BEHIND THE DATA

This activity provides children with a simple introduction to irreversible chemical reactions, and is an important introduction to the chemical changes they will study in secondary school.

Most chemical reactions are similar to the reaction of plaster of Paris with water: they give out heat (are exothermic). More energy is released when making new chemical bonds in the product than is required to break the existing chemical bonds in the starting materials (the reactants). The excess energy is lost to the surroundings. Where chemical reactions occur quickly, as in the reaction of metals with acids, the mixture often becomes hot. The burning of carbon-based materials (reacting with oxygen under initial conditions of intense heat) releases a lot of energy, which is why we burn fuels to provide heat and drive machines.

Adding acids to the carbonates or hydrogen carbonates of metals produces the gas carbon dioxide. The reaction of sodium hydrogen carbonate with citric acid is unusual in that it absorbs heat from the surroundings (it is endothermic). More energy is required to break the bonds in the reactants than is produced when new bonds are formed in the products (sodium citrate, carbon dioxide and water).

When you are discussing irreversible changes with the children and asking them to make predictions about whether the temperature will rise or fall, it is always important to value both predictions. The children will find out in secondary school that either answer can be right, depending on the reactants.

Answers
1. About 5 minutes.
2. It took some time for the reaction between the water and the plaster of Paris to start happening – this is quite a slow reaction.
3. 37°C
4. 17°C
5. It would cool down to room temperature (20°C).
6. At about 5½ minutes.
7. 2°C
8. 11°C
9. Yes, irreversible changes often cause an energy change. They can either release heat so that the temperature rises (as in Investigation 1), or take in heat so that it falls (Investigation 2).
10. The reaction of plaster of Paris with water took about 40 minutes. The reaction of baking powder with citric acid solution took less than 1 minute, so it was much faster than the first reaction.

Irreversible changes

Class 6 were looking at irreversible changes. Sachin and Anul decided to see what happened when they added water to plaster of Paris powder, measuring any temperature changes that occurred with a datalogger. Mytili and Ana did the same investigation using baking powder and citric acid solution.

Investigation 1: Sachin and Anul observed that the white plaster of Paris powder had become very hard an hour after mixing. This graph shows the changes in temperature.

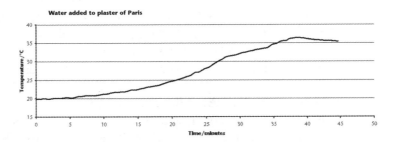

Questions

1. How many minutes was it before the temperature started to change?
2. Why do you think the temperature did not change immediately?
3. What was the highest temperature reached?
4. What was the increase in temperature?
5. What would happen to the temperature if the mixture was left for another hour?

Investigation 2: Mytili and Ana observed that a lot of fizzing happened when the baking powder was added. This graph shows the changes in temperature. They made sure they had a steady temperature before they added the baking powder.

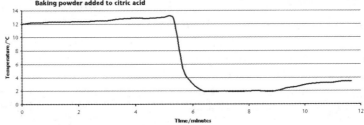

6. When do you think the baking powder was dropped into the citric acid?
7. What was the lowest temperature reached?
8. What was the decrease in temperature?
9. Do energy changes happen during an irreversible change? Explain your answer.
10. Look at the two graphs. How long did each reaction take? Which reaction was the faster of the two?

BETTER CONDUCTORS

National Curriculum Science KS2 PoS Sc4: 1a, b, c
QCA Science Unit 6G: Changing circuits
Scottish 5–14 Guidelines Science Properties and uses of energy – Level C

HOW TO GATHER THE DATA

This activity can be done using simple equipment, as long as you have a datalogger. You may not get exactly the results given here, because other factors will affect the readings – especially how good the contact on the metal strip is. Cleaning the contact points with emery cloth will help. Different brands of datalogger respond differently to low light levels, so you may have to screen your bulb and sensor to stop light from other sources affecting the results.

THE SCIENCE BEHIND THE DATA

All materials are made from atoms. An atom consists of a nucleus orbited by electrons. Electricity flows when the electrons move from atom to atom. Metals have a structure that allows the electrons to flow easily from one atom to another, but non-metals do not (they produce static electricity). Carbon (graphite), used in pencil leads, is an exception: a non-metal that conducts electricity. In a circuit, the metal components all contain free electrons. When a battery is connected in the circuit, all the electrons flow in the same direction (from the negative terminal and through the circuit to the positive terminal). Although all metals are conductors of electricity, some are better than others: silver is the best, lead is not very good.

The ability to allow electrons through is called conductance; being relatively difficult for electrons to pass through is called resistance. Some metals (such as lead, tin and iron) have a higher resistance than others (such as aluminium, copper and silver). As electricity passes through a material, it carries energy with it. The battery releases electrons with higher energy than those returning to the battery. As they move round, some of this energy is transferred to the surroundings – which is why electrical circuits often become warm. A lot of the energy is released in the bulb when it lights up. The electrical elements of heaters and bulbs are designed to have a high resistance, so a lot of energy is released as electrons pass through them – so the component gives out heat and/or light. The rate of energy loss is the power of the circuit (measured in watts). I always discourage children from talking about 'power' coming from a battery: what flows from the battery is electricity.

Copper is used for domestic wiring: it is a good conductor, so the energy loss is minimal. Aluminium is used for overhead cables: it is a slightly less good conductor than copper, but weighs less.

Answers

1. A material that lets electricity pass through it.
2. The five metals tested are very different, and there are no intermediate values. Data of this kind are called discrete (separate) data. If a graph has words along the x-axis and numbers up the y-axis, it is usually showing discrete data and so needs to be a bar graph. If the graph has numbers on both axes, it is showing 'continuous data' and so needs to be be a line graph.
3. Copper
4. Lead
5. 400 lux
6. Steel
7. Aluminium and copper.
8. They are both good conductors of electricity.
9.

Metal	Brightness/lux
copper	650
aluminium	400
zinc	170
steel	88
lead	50

10. Diagram as shown on right.

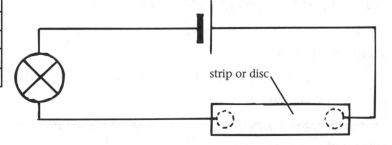

strip or disc

Better conductors

Cavin and Tony were testing different materials to see whether they conducted electricity. By using their circuit, they found that all the metals conducted electricity – but sometimes, the bulb was not as bright. They asked their teacher whether they could investigate further, and she let them use a datalogger to measure the brightness of the bulb each time.

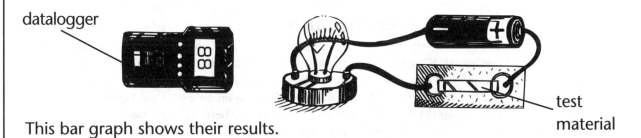

datalogger

test material

This bar graph shows their results.

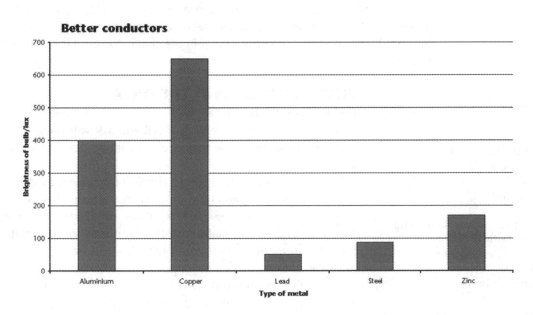

Questions

1. What is a conductor?

2. Why did the children plot a bar graph and not a line graph?

3. Which metal produced the brightest bulb?

4. Which metal produced the dimmest bulb?

5. What was the brightness of the bulb for aluminium?

6. Which metal is being tested by the datalogger in the diagram?

7. Which two metals would be good for making electrical wires?

8. Explain your answer to Question 7.

9. Draw a table to show the brightness of the bulbs for the five conductors, in order from the best conductor to the poorest conductor.

10. Draw Cavin and Tony's test circuit using electrical circuit symbols.

LONGER WIRES

National Curriculum Science KS2 PoS Sc4: 1a, b, c
QCA Science Unit 6G: Changing circuits
Scottish 5–14 Guidelines Science Properties and uses of
energy – Level D

HOW TO GATHER THE DATA

You can demonstrate this relationship by using a datalogger to measure the brightness of a bulb, but you will need to match the type of resistance wire and the power rating on the bulb to obtain a visible effect. The method shown opposite is simpler, but you will need to have an ammeter (or borrow one from a friendly secondary school). This investigation was done with 125 swg Constantan wire (again, a secondary school will have plenty) and a 3.5V, 2A bulb. If you use the resistance wire on its own, you need to take care that the current is not too high, as the wire can become very hot and even glow red. This should not happen if the right bulb is in the circuit, because the bulb will blow first.

Answers

1. 30cm
2. 40cm
3. It does not fit the pattern: it is slightly too high.
4. (A smooth curve drawn through the points, but missing out the suspect value. If they connect all the points, discuss with the children why they have included that reading when they suspected it was wrong.)
5. 1.5 amps (or just less)
6. 1.4 amps
7. Between 0.9 and 1.0 amps.
8.

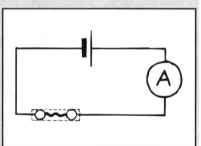

9. Kept the wire straight, checked that the zero mark on the ruler was at the start of the wire, placed the clips as close to the ends of the wire as possible.
10. The longer the wire, the less current flows in the circuit. This happens because a longer wire has more resistance to the flow of electricity.

THE SCIENCE BEHIND THE DATA

We have used the familiar terms 'battery' and 'bulb' here. Strictly speaking, a 1.5 volt 'battery' is a cell and a 9 volt battery is a collection of six cells. The correct electrical term for a 'bulb' is a lamp.

The flow of electricity around a circuit is the flow of electrons: negatively charged particles from the metal atoms. The current is the rate of flow of these particles. If you use the word *current* with the children, explain that the ammeter measures the current. Alternatively, you could talk about the rate at which electrical charge passes a given point in the circuit.

A chemical reaction in the battery releases electrons with higher energy than those returning to the battery. As the electrons move around, some of this energy is transferred from the circuit to the surroundings, which is why electrical elements often heat up. The more batteries you have, the harder the electricity is 'pushed', so the higher the current and the greater the amount of heat and light produced by the bulb. The amount of 'push' in a circuit is measured in volts. It depends on the number of batteries and the chemicals in the battery.

When electricity passes through any component, there is resistance to its flow. The longer or thinner the wire, the higher the resistance of that component – and so the more quickly energy is lost from it. The brightness of a bulb depends on the resistance of the filament wire and the current passing through it. If the resistance of the filament is high, it becomes hot and bright. The light and heat transfer energy from the bulb to the surroundings. More batteries will push more electricity around the circuit, so energy is transferred more quickly, making the bulb brighter and hotter. If the filament gets too hot, it melts and breaks the circuit.

Longer wires

Salma asked whether using a longer wire made it more difficult for electricity to pass through it – "because if you put two bulbs in a circuit, they are dimmer." She tried using three crocodile leads instead of one, and couldn't see any difference. Her teacher said she needed a special kind of wire to make a difference: it needed to be like the wire that heats up in a toaster.

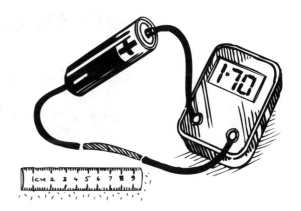

Salma set up a circuit like the one shown in the diagram, and used an ammeter to measure the current going around the circuit when she used different lengths of a special wire.

This is a graph of her results.

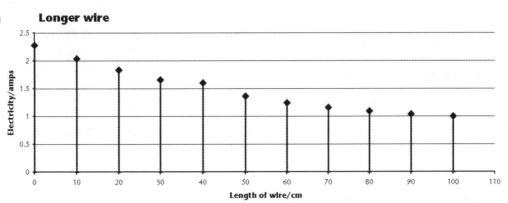

Questions

1. In the diagram, which length of wire was being used? Look at the reading on the ammeter.

2. Which reading do you think Salma should try again?

3. Explain your answer to Question 2.

4. Draw a smooth line on the graph to show the trend.

5. Look at the reading you suggested Salma should try again. What do you think this reading should have been?

6. What was the meter reading for a 50cm length of wire?

7. What do you think would be the reading for 110cm of wire?

8. Draw a circuit diagram for Salma's testing circuit.

9. Suggest two things that she should have done to make sure her results were reliable.

10. How does the length of the wire affect the current going through the circuit? Can you explain why?

HANDLING SCIENCE DATA YEAR 6

LOTS OF BATTERIES

> **National Curriculum Science** KS2 PoS Sc4: 1a, b, c
> **QCA Science** Unit 6G: Changing circuits
> **Scottish 5–14 Guidelines Science** Properties and uses of energy – Level D

HOW TO GATHER THE DATA

This activity can be done using simple equipment, as long as you have a datalogger. You should get exactly this shape of curve if your batteries are not run down. You could deliberately include one old battery and ask the children to explain why it does not increase the brightness by as much as the others. This activity is excellent as part of a group discussion, with the children doing different tasks under your supervision. These simple activities are also a good way for you to become confident with datalogging – for example, an NQT who had never even seen this software or equipment before had a 15-minute training session and then did this activity during an inspection week. Different brands of datalogger respond differently to low light levels, so you may need to screen your bulb and sensor to prevent light from other sources getting in and affecting the results.

THE SCIENCE BEHIND THE DATA

See 'Longer wires' (page 46) for an explanation of how batteries and bulbs work. The more batteries are connected, the more electricity is 'pushed' around the circuit, so the higher the current – and so the higher the *rate* at which the bulb produces heat and light as a consequence of its resistance to the current. The rate of energy release is the power (measured in watts). The relationship between power and number of batteries produces a curved graph. If the filament becomes too hot, it melts and breaks the circuit.

When the battery 'runs out', it is not the electricity that has run out: it is the energy of the electrons. The electricity is still there, but the battery cannot 'push' it around the circuit. The chemical releasing high-energy electrons has been used up, so there is no energy difference (no 'push') to make the electrons flow. A rechargeable battery is made from chemicals that can be reformed by 'pushing' electricity in the opposite direction. It is 're-energised' so that the battery can 'push' electricity around the circuit again.

This explanation is not required for this age group – but Year 6 children are quite capable of exploring these ideas with suitable investigations to provide the evidence, and it gives them a much clearer understanding of electricity.

Answers

1.

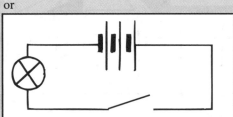

or

2.

Number of batteries	Brightness of bulb/ lux

3. If there is no battery, the bulb will not light at all.

4. 300 lux

5. No, because the bulb is still lit.

6. About 1600 lux.

7. The more batteries, the brighter the bulb (as long as it does not blow from overheating).

8. Using more batteries provides a bigger push (more voltage). More electricity is pushed around, so the energy is released more quickly. (Children should give this response with some further questioning to help them.)

9. No. For example, 3 batteries gives just over 100 lux, but 6 batteries gives about 1060 lux. Doubling the number of batteries gives about 10 times the brightness.

Lots of batteries

Class 6 were having a discussion about batteries. Miss Ford asked: "What happens if I put another battery in the circuit?"

"We don't know, Miss!" was the answer. They did really: they just wanted to see whether Miss Ford would blow the bulb. She used a datalogger to measure the brightness of the bulb each time she added a battery.

This is a graph of the results.

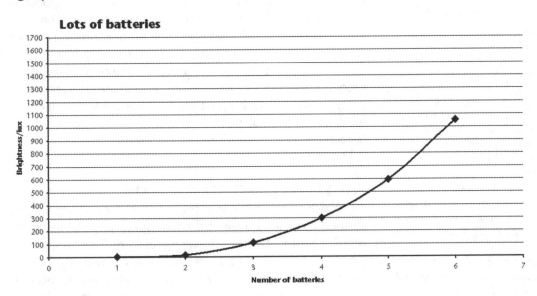

Questions

1. Draw a circuit that Miss Ford might have used for three batteries, a bulb and a switch. You can draw a picture or a circuit diagram.

2. Design a table the children could use to write their results in.

3. The brightness with 1 battery was 3 lux. Why does the graph not go lower than 1 battery?

4. What is the brightness with 4 batteries?

5. Did Miss Ford blow the bulb? How can you tell?

6. How bright do you think the bulb will be with 7 batteries?

7. How does the number of batteries affect the brightness of the bulb?

8. Explain your answer to Question 7 scientifically.

9. Does doubling the number of batteries double the brightness? Use values from the graph to justify your answer.

HANDLING SCIENCE DATA YEAR 6

HELICOPTERS

> **National Curriculum Science** KS2 PoS Sc4: 2b, c
> **QCA Science** Unit 6E: Forces in action
> **Scottish 5–14 Guidelines Science** Forces and their effects – Levels C, D

HOW TO GATHER THE DATA

You will need stopwatches or timers that measure to the nearest 0.01s for this activity, or you will not measure any difference. If you wish, you can ignore the decimal point and ask the children just to record the digits with the units 'hundredths of a second'. However, children are expected to work with numbers to two decimal places by the end of Year 5 (Level D for Primary 6/7).

This is a good activity to encourage co-ordination and teamwork. The children need to start and stop the watch at exactly the right times, and this will need a clear method and allocation of roles (for example, one child to drop the helicopter, one to say something like '3, 2, 1, go!', someone to start and stop the watch at the correct points, and someone to record the result. It also illustrates the importance of having a consistent procedure. We suggest a 3m drop as a minimum; stairwells are ideal for dropping the helicopters, but this needs to be done safely and under strict supervision. Several publications contain templates for paper helicopters, and there is one in the Wizards section of *Microsoft Publisher* ('Whirlybird airplane').

THE SCIENCE BEHIND THE DATA

You may be able to see that the helicopter speeds up when it is released and then travels at a steady speed until it hits the floor, when it stops. The helicopter would continue to speed up (accelerate) if air resistance did not slow it down. The faster the helicopter travels, the greater the air resistance that it encounters, until it reaches a terminal velocity at which the forces are balanced: the weight of the helicopter is balanced by the air resistance pushing up, so its speed remains constant. If the forces were unbalanced, it would either speed up or slow down, depending on which force was greater.

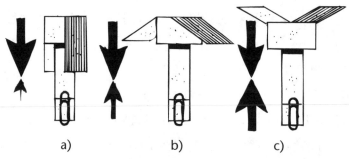

a)   b)   c)

a) parachute closed, weight > air resistance, parachute accelerates
b) parachute opens, air resistance increases, parachute accelerates less
c) weight and air resistance are balanced, parachute falls at a steady speed.

Answers

1. (A completed stick graph.)
2. Longer
3. Slower
4. (A point on the graph at the same height as for 7–10 clips.)
5. From 7–10 paper clips the graph is a horizontal line, so adding more paper clips will probably make no difference. The brighter children might appreciate that this is only a strong probability, not a certainty. Some children might draw the stick lower, even at zero (perhaps because it is the last one). Discuss with them why they chose that value.
6. A point near 260 hundredths of a second (between 250 and 300 is reasonable).
7. The value can be predicted by extending the curve back to the axis. (Be prepared for logical alternatives, such as 'It won't spin properly with no clips' – this is sometimes the case.)
8. Same material for helicopter, same helicopter size, dropped from same height, held with fingers at same place (the top is best), paper clips of same size or mass.
9. The children could investigate any idea given in response to Question 8. The type of material would probably have an unpredictable effect. The children could predict the effect of size: bigger wings will give more air resistance (however, there is an optimum wing length). If they change the paper clips, it may be difficult to separate the effects of size and of mass.

Helicopters

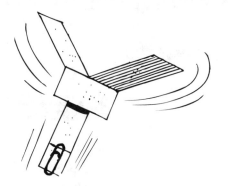

Some children did an investigation with paper helicopters. These helicopters spin round very quickly and fall slowly.

The children wanted to know whether they would fall faster if they were loaded with paper clips. They put one paper clip on a helicopter and measured how long it took to fall. Then they added another and measured the time again. They did this until they had added 10 paper clips.

They plotted their results on a graph.

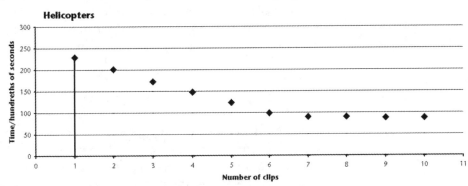

Questions

1. Draw a vertical line down from each point on the graph to the axis to make a stick graph. The first one has been done for you.

2. Is the time for 2 paper clips **shorter** or **longer** than for 4 paper clips?

3. Is the speed for 2 paper clips **faster** or **slower** than for 4 paper clips?

4. Draw a stick on the graph to predict the result for 12 paper clips.

5. Explain your prediction.

6. Draw a stick on the graph for 0 paper clips.

7. Explain your answer to Question 6.

8. Describe three things that the children should have done to make their investigation a fair test.

9. Think of and plan another investigation using a paper helicopter. Include these things in your plan:

- what you are trying to find out (your question)
- what you will change each time
- what you will measure each time
- what you will keep the same each time
- a prediction about what will happen
- a blank table showing the headings and units
- a blank graph showing the labelled axes
- a prediction about what the graph will look like.

PARACHUTES

National Curriculum Science KS2 PoS Sc4: 2c
QCA Science Unit 6E: Forces in action
Scottish 5–14 Guidelines Science Forces and their effects – Level E

HOW TO GATHER THE DATA

Parachutes provide a rich opportunity for investigative work, as there are many factors that can be tested. For this activity, you will need stopwatches or timers that measure to the nearest 0.01s – otherwise, you will not be able to measure any difference. You can ignore the decimal point and just record the digits if you wish – or you can use it as an exercise in working with decimals. The mass used with the parachutes should be the minimum needed for a steady fall; the same object should be used each time.

This is a good exercise in co-ordination and teamwork. The children need to start and stop the watch at exactly the right times, and this will need a clear method and allocation of roles (for example: one child to drop the parachute, one to say something like '3, 2, 1, go!', one to start and stop the watch, and one to record the results. Emphasise the importance of having a consistent procedure. The greater the height the parachute is dropped from the better (we suggest 3m minimum), but this needs to be done safely. Also, how the parachute is held when dropping it is important. The best place to hold for it to open well is the very top.

A lot of science is involved in understanding the results. The children may be able to see that the parachute speeds up when first released (until it opens) and then travels at a steady speed until it hits the floor. They can learn to discard unreliable results (such as when the parachute does not open properly).

THE SCIENCE BEHIND THE DATA

The process by which the parachute accelerates towards a terminal velocity and then continues to fall at that velocity is described in 'Helicopters' (page 50). The most important point to remember is that the parachute does not slow down when it opens: it just accelerates less and less, until its velocity is constant. The downward force of its weight, caused by gravity, is opposed by the upward force of air resistance. If you did this investigation on the Moon, where there is no atmosphere, the parachute would continue to accelerate until it hit the ground.

The graph shows that there is an optimum size for a parachute to delay the falling of a given mass. If the parachute is too small, there is only a small upward force of air resistance. If the parachute is too large, its weight will prevent it from opening properly, so again the air resistance will be lower than the optimum.

Answers

1. 30cm and 35cm
2. 5cm and 50cm
3. 5s
4. 32.5cm
5. This value is midway between 30cm and 35cm, the two parachutes that took the longest to fall.
6. a) As the size of the parachute increases, the air resistance or drag increases, so the time to fall becomes longer. b) The parachute becomes too heavy to open properly, so the air resistance does not increase as much.
7. Balanced
8. Any two of: same material, same height, same way of dropping, same shape.
9. Any of the factors listed in Question 8 could be investigated, or the children might think of others. The appropriate sections of the planning board (photocopiable pages 62 and 63) should be completed.

Parachutes

Class 6 were testing parachutes to see whether the size of the parachute affected the time taken for it to fall. Each group made a different-sized parachute and measured the diameter.

This is a graph of their results.

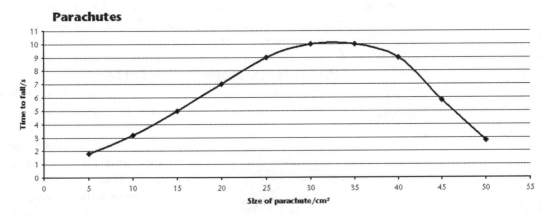

Questions

1. Which two parachutes took the longest time to fall?

2. Which two parachutes fell the fastest?

3. How long did the 15cm parachute take to fall?

4. What would be the exact best size for a parachute to delay the falling of the mass used in the experiment?

5. Use the data on the graph to explain your answer to Question 4.

6. Explain why the graph shows a pattern of **a)** increasing time, then **b)** decreasing time to fall as the size of the parachute increases.

7. When the parachute is falling at a steady speed, are the forces acting on it balanced or unbalanced?

8. Name two things the children should have done to make the investigation fair.

9. Think of another factor to do with parachutes that the children could investigate. Write a full plan for the investigation. In your plan, you should include:

■ what you will change each time

■ what you will measure each time

■ what you will keep the same each time

■ a blank table for your results, showing the headings and units

■ a blank graph for your results (label the axes correctly and give the units).

HANDLING SCIENCE DATA YEAR 6

HOW FAR THE CAR GOES

National Curriculum Science KS2 PoS Sc4: 2c
QCA Science Unit 6E: Forces in action
Scottish 5–14 Guidelines Science Forces and their effects – Levels C, E

HOW TO GATHER THE DATA

Rolling a toy car down a ramp is a fairly simple exercise. The children can use a tape measure to work out the distance travelled. You can make a simple, cheap, adjustable ramp using corroflute (see diagram on resource page 64).

THE SCIENCE BEHIND THE DATA

The early questions can be used to assess children's ability to plot a line graph. The data-handling skills needed for the later questions are much higher-order, and you should only attempt them with children who have proved themselves to be very competent with a range of data-handling skills in previous activities.

Gravity pulls the toy car down the ramp. Since gravity is acting all the time that the car is on the ramp, the car speeds up (accelerates) throughout this time. The longer the car is on the ramp, the faster it will be travelling when it leaves the ramp and the further it will travel beyond the ramp. The friction between the surface of the ramp and the cars' wheels, and between the axles and the wheels, slows the car down and makes it stop. The greater the friction, the shorter the distance travelled by the car.

The mass of the car needs to be kept constant in this investigation. It will not affect how fast the car travels, since a heavier car will accelerate at the same rate under gravity as a lighter one. (If you drop a tennis ball and a cricket or hockey ball at the same time, from one hand, they will land together.) However, a heavier car will travel further from the ramp, because it has more momentum: it is able to keep going further against friction. Imagine catching a football: it will hit your hands harder, and so take more effort to hold onto, than a tennis ball thrown at the same speed.

Answers

1. A line graph as shown:

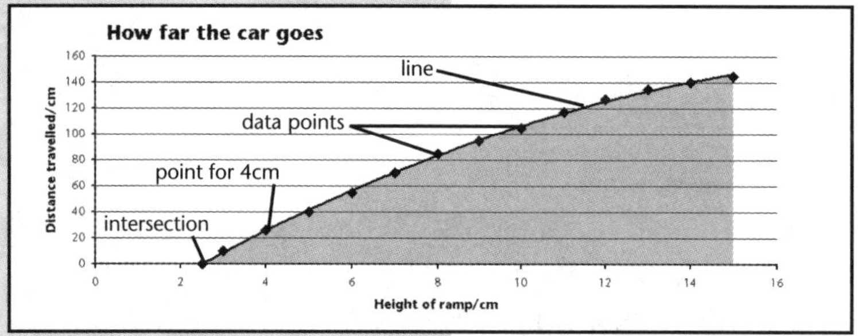

The child should draw a line of best fit. The intersection should be added for Question 4. The shaded area relates to the answer for Question 8.)

2. It is a smooth curved line (or any other point the child can justify).

3. About 28cm

4. (An extension of the curve giving an intersection around 2.3cm.)

5. Letting go in the same way, same starting position on the ramp, same surface under the ramp. (Not the same ruler, since this is standard.)

6. a) Gravity **b)** Friction

7. The car would go further for each height of the ramp. Encourage the children to be precise: 'further' is more precise than 'more', 'bigger' or 'higher'. Also, saying 'for each height of the ramp' makes it clear that only the surface is being changed.

8. (Points and a curve drawn anywhere in the shaded area on the graph. The curve might be steeper than the one derived from the actual results, but it should certainly be higher if the answer to Question 7 is correct.)

How far the car goes

Laura, Samantha and Ben were trying to find out whether a car on a ramp would go further if they used a steeper slope. They set up a ramp like the one shown in the picture and let a car run down it. They measured how far the car travelled before it stopped. Then they set the ramp to different heights and measured the distance travelled each time.

This is their table of results.

car ramp height/cm	distance travelled/cm
15	145
14	140
13	135
12	127
11	117
10	105
9	95
8	85
7	70
6	55
5	40

Questions

1. Plot a line graph of the children's results. Remember to draw the line of best fit and label your axes with the correct units.

2. What do you notice about the line you have drawn?

3. Predict what the distance will be for a ramp 4cm high.

4. Continue the line down to zero on the axis that shows the distance travelled.

5. Name three things the children should have been careful about to make this a fair test.

6. Name **a)** the force that causes the car to move down the ramp and **b)** the force that causes the car to stop.

7. This investigation was carried out on a carpet. How would you expect the results to be different if a smooth tiled floor were used?

8. Imagine the sort of results you might get on a smooth tiled floor. Draw some points on the graph to show this, then draw a line through your points.

HANDLING SCIENCE DATA YEAR 6

WHAT SHOULD I WEAR AT NIGHT?

> **National Curriculum Science** KS2 PoS Sc4: 3a, c, d
> **QCA Science** Unit 6F: How we see things
> **Scottish 5–14 Guidelines Science** Properties and uses of energy – Level C

HOW TO GATHER THE DATA

There are several ways of obtaining this type of graph. A simple way is to paint a shoebox black inside, cut a small hole in one end to see through and cut a 5–7cm slit in the lid. (See SPACE research reports (1990), *Light,* Liverpool University Press.) Attach an aluminium foil shape to the back wall inside the box. If the children look through the hole with the slit shut, they will not see anything. If they open the slit, light will enter the box and be reflected from the foil into their eyes – ask them why they can now see the shiny shape. Repeat this using different-coloured materials; the children should begin to group colours that reflect light well and colours that do not. Placing a light probe in the hole to act as an 'eye' allows us to make quantitative comparisons between colours.

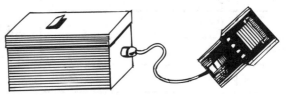

Answers

1. Aluminium foil.
2. It has a very shiny surface, like a mirror.
3. Black
4. Yes. If a surface reflects light, it stops (blocks) the light, so the light does not pass through it. (Judge the answer and the explanation together.)
5. The light colours: white and yellow.
6. The dark colours: black and brown.
7. The car's headlights produce light rays which hit the surface of your body and reflect back into the driver's eyes so that he can see you. (A diagram showing rays with arrows pointing from a car's headlights to a child, then from the child into the car driver's eyes.)
8. Light colours such as white.
9. Between 15% and 20% would be a good prediction. The actual value is 16%.
10. Most of the light is absorbed, which is why you feel hot wearing black on a sunny day (and cooler wearing white).

THE SCIENCE BEHIND THE DATA

You need to revise the topic of how we see things in Year 6, as it is difficult for children to accept that we see objects because light from a source reflects from the object into our eyes. In a study of over 400 15-year-old children's ideas about vision (Ramadas and Driver (1989), *Secondary children's ideas about light,* Children's Learning in Science Project, University of Leeds), 31% thought that light rays went from the book to the eye; 12% thought light simply helped us to see better; 19% thought the eye was 'active' in some way; and 9% thought something went from the eye to the book. So misconceptions about how we see things are persistent, despite efforts to overcome these through teaching.

If there is no light source, we cannot see things. If a surface scatters light by reflecting it in many directions, no image is reflected. A mirror reflects all the light at the same angle, so the image remains intact. When the children are drawing light ray diagrams, encourage them to use a ruler: light travels in straight lines. The lines should touch the light source and the object's surface.

Go on to discuss which colours reflect light the best. Ask the children how drivers can see us at night, why car headlights appear to 'reach' further at night, and what colours are best to wear at night for safety purposes. (Which groups of workers need reflective clothing?) Organisations such as RoSPA will often provide samples of special materials that are used to produce reflective clothing.

What should I wear at night?

A Year 6 class were revising light and how we see things. Chloe, Matt and Simi decided to find out whether some colours are easier to see than others. They used a light probe attached to a datalogger to measure how much light was reflected from different-coloured surfaces.

They recorded their results in a bar graph. The datalogger recorded the amount of light reflected as a percentage of bright daylight.

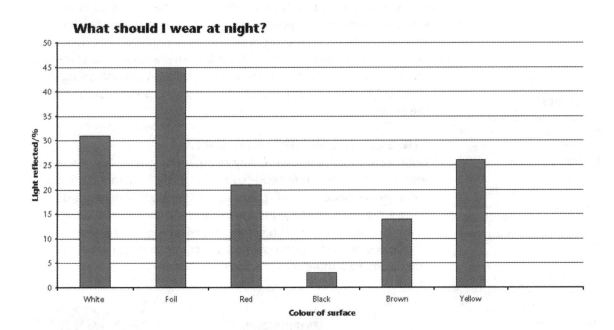

Questions

1. Which surface reflected the most light?

2. Why do you think this surface reflected the most light?

3. Which surface reflected the least light?

4. Do you think these surfaces are opaque? Explain your answer.

5. Which colours are good at reflecting light?

6. Which colours are poor at reflecting light?

7. Explain scientifically how a car driver can see you on a dark night. Draw a diagram to help you.

8. What colours should you wear so that drivers can see you more easily?

9. Predict how much light a purple surface will reflect. Draw your prediction in the space on the bar chart. Don't forget to add a label.

10. What happens to light when it hits a dark surface?

SHADOW PUPPET

> **National Curriculum Science** KS2 PoS Sc4: 3a, b
> **QCA Science** Unit 6F: How we see things
> **Scottish 5–14 Guidelines Science** Properties and uses of energy – Level C

HOW TO GATHER THE DATA

An OHP is a good light source for this investigation. All the children can participate in this simple activity, as there are many jobs to do. Ask the children to predict the next reading each time – they can all have a try to start with. This encourages them to analyse the data as they investigate, basing their predictions on the trend of the previous results. The more data they have gathered, the more refined their predictions become. Because the context is simple, this activity can be used to refine children's investigating skills – particularly their measuring skills (for example, good alignment with the zero mark on the tape measure).

THE SCIENCE BEHIND THE DATA

Light travels in straight lines. Any opaque object will cast a shadow with the same shape as the object, because the light cannot go through the object or bend around it. The size of the shadow depends on the relative positions of the light source, the object and the surface on which the shadow falls. This can be modelled for the children using a small piece of plastic with holes in each corner and four art straws (or you can make a more robust wooden version):

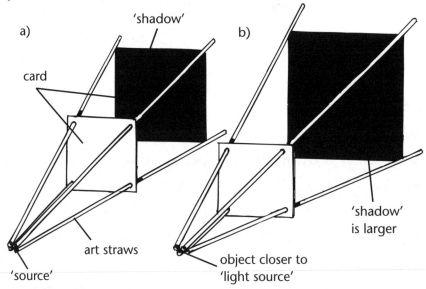

The size of the shadow depends upon the angle made by the light rays from the source. As the source moves towards the object, this angle increases. It is not a linear change: it changes as a proportion of distance between object and source. For example, if the distance is 20cm and the object moves 1cm, there is a $1/20$ change (5%) in the size of the shadow. If the distance is 5cm and the source moves by 1cm, there is a $1/5$ change (20%) in the size of the shadow.

Answers

1. It is opaque, it blocks the light, or the light cannot get through it.
2. 75cm and 19cm
3. 10cm
4. The shadow can never be any smaller than the object.
5. The nearer the puppet is to the lamp, the larger the shadow. (For notes on comparative statements, see the Introduction, page 6.)
6. (Look for straight lines, drawn carefully with a ruler, and arrow marks indicating that light travels from the lamp to the top and bottom of the puppet and on to the top and bottom of the shadow.)
7. Distance between lamp and screen, height of puppet, brightness of lamp. (Not the ruler, because this is standard.)
8. Several answers are possible, including: when the Sun shines, when the Moon 'shines' (reflects), when the streetlamps are on. Ask questions to explore each answer. *Do you have a shadow in the shade?* (No, because the light there is too scattered.) *Does the Moon give out light?* (No, it reflects light from the Sun.) *What happens if you stand halfway between two streetlamps?* (You will have two shadows, one from each lamp.)

Shadow puppet

Class 6 were wondering how it is that the size of a shadow can change, but you can still tell what it is making the shadow.

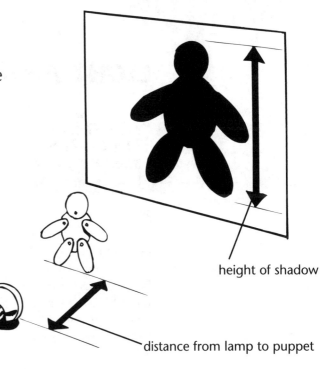

height of shadow

They set up an investigation. They shone a lamp at a puppet and measured the height of its shadow on a screen. They moved the puppet further away from the lamp and measured the height of the shadow again. They did this for ten distances.

distance from lamp to puppet

They drew a graph to show their results.

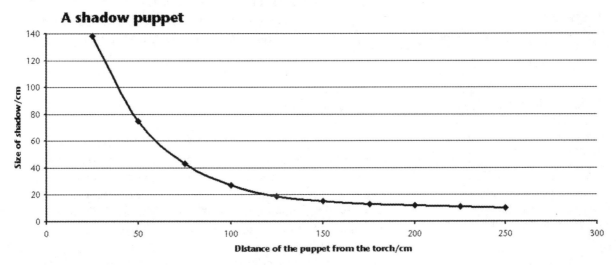

Questions

1. Why does the puppet cause a shadow on the screen?

2. What is the height of the shadow when the puppet is **a)** 50cm and **b)** 125cm from the lamp?

3. How high will the shadow be when the puppet is 300cm from the lamp?

4. Why can the shadow never be 0cm high?

5. Describe how the height of the shadow changes as the puppet is moved further away from the lamp.

6. Draw lines on the diagram at the top of the page to show how the light travels to make the shadow on the screen.

7. What two things should have been kept the same to make the test fair?

8. We sometimes have a shadow outdoors. When does this happen?

HANDLING SCIENCE DATA YEAR 6

LIGHT AND DISTANCE

> *National Curriculum Science* KS2 PoS Sc4: 1a, 3a
> *QCA Science* Unit 6F: How we see things
> *Scottish 5–14 Guidelines Science* Properties and uses of energy –
> Level C; Earth in space – Level C

HOW TO GATHER THE DATA

This is a quick and simple investigation, but it shows children the importance of taking care with their technique so that they get reliable results. The investigation was carried out using a LogIT Explorer, because it does not register low light levels: the activity could be done in a classroom with the lights turned off. The light source was a simple battery and bulb circuit. It is a good idea to use a bit of Blu-Tack or Sellotape to stop the bulb holder moving, and to attach the metre ruler to the table to act as a guide for alignment as well as a measuring instrument. Make sure the sensor and bulb are correctly lined up, both vertically and horizontally.

THE SCIENCE BEHIND THE DATA

This activity will help to build up the children's understanding of light. It demonstrates that light travels from a source and becomes less intense the further you are from the source. A parallel can be drawn with the way that sounds are less loud further from the source. The children probably know that if we travelled in space nearer to the Sun, the light and heat would become too intense for us to survive. Some stars that are much brighter than our Sun are only just visible, because they are millions of light years away. The light becomes less intense because it radiates out from the source, covering the area of a sphere. If the sphere is bigger (at a greater distance from the light source), the light intensity is less. (Think of a hedgehog: the spines are closer together nearer to the skin.)

The graph shows a curve because the light intensity depends on the area of a sphere ($4\pi r^2$ where r is the radius). Light intensity decreases in proportion to the increase in the radius squared (r^2) – see diagram on right.

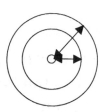

Answers

1. A line graph as shown below. The extension for 80cm is the answer to Question 4.
2. It is a smooth curve, with all the points fitting on the line.
3. The nearer the light source, the brighter the light. (For notes on comparative statements, see the Introduction, page 6.)
4. See extension in graph below.
5. About 35 lux.
6. About 180 lux (look for correct use of the line graph).
7. Same batteries, same bulb, bulb in same position, same alignment of datalogger. (Not the same ruler, as this is standard.)
8. The readings would be higher for the same distances from the bulb. Encourage precise answers – for example, talking about the readings, not the brightness of the bulb. Saying 'for the same distances from the bulb' makes it clear that this aspect of the experiment is not changed.
9. Some of the major points are: Connect the batteries and the bulb in the circuit to make the bulb light up. Line up the datalogger light sensor with the bulb. Set up the datalogger 10cm from the bulb and take the brightness reading. Move the datalogger to 20cm from the bulb and take another reading. Repeat for distances up to 70cm.

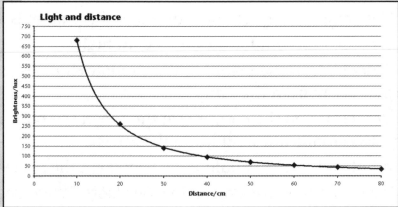

Light and distance

Class 6 were investigating all sorts of things about light. Gary and Ian were using a datalogger to find out whether the brightness of a bulb was the same at different distances from it. Here is is a photograph of how they did it.

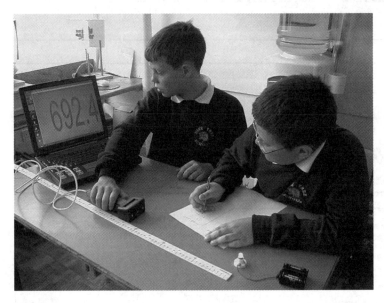

Here are their results.

Distance/cm	Brightness/lux
10	680
20	260
30	140
40	95
50	70
60	55
70	45

Questions

1. Plot a line graph of Gary and Ian's results. Remember to draw the line and label your axes with the correct units.

2. What do you notice about the line you have drawn?

3. Describe how the brightness of the light changes with the distance from the light source.

4. Extend the line graph to show the brightness at 80cm.

5. What do you predict the brightness to be at this distance?

6. Use the curve to predict a value for the brightness of the bulb at 25cm.

7. Name three things the children should have kept the same to make this a fair test.

8. What would happen to their readings if they connected an extra battery into the circuit?

9. Write out a set of instructions to tell someone else how to do the investigation that Gary and Ian have done.

HANDLING SCIENCE DATA YEAR 6

Our planning board

Our question is: _____

_____

Our prediction is: _____

_____

We will change:

We will measure:

We will keep these things the same:

Our table

We will measure:					
We will change:					

Our graph

We will
measure:

We will
change:

Graph axes

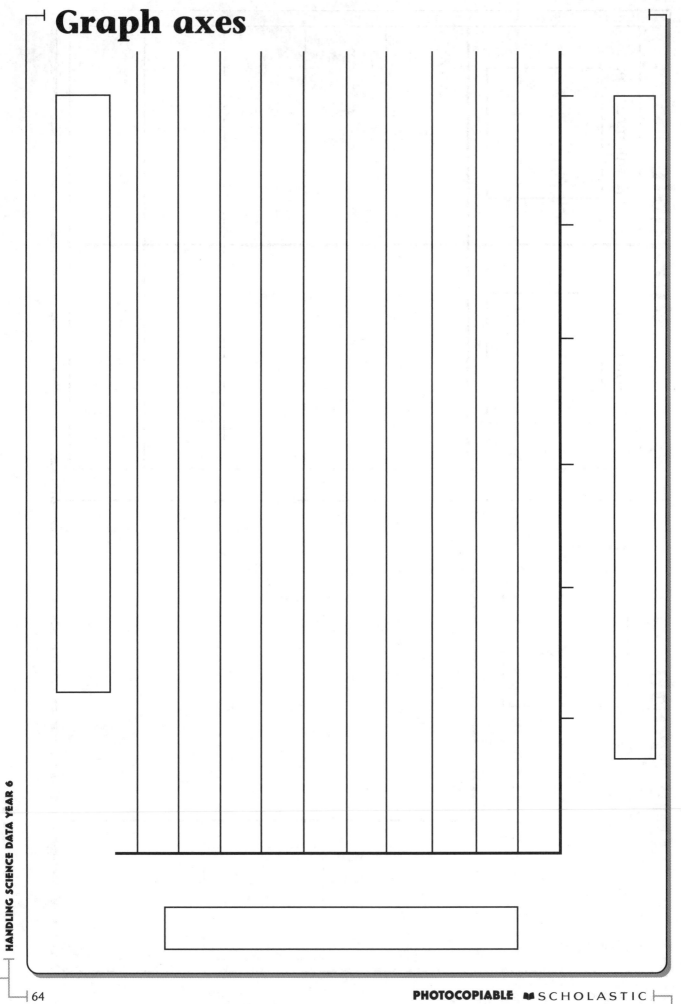